THE SALARYMAN

A MEMOIR

Michael Howard
Illustrated by Rena Saiya

Copyright © 2019 Michael Howard
Illustrations by Rena Saiya
Print Edition

All rights reserved.

Parts of Chapters 3, 7 and 12, in somewhat different form, first appeared on the CNN Travel blog. The author's previous blog, The Manner Mode, also published some portions of this book.

No part of this publication may be reproduced, distributed, or transmitted in any form or by any means, including photocopying, recording, or other electronic or mechanical methods, without the prior written permission of the publisher, except in the case of brief quotations embodied in critical reviews and certain other noncommercial uses permitted by copyright law. For permissions or inquiries, please contact michael@thesalarymanbook.com.

Cover illustration: Rena Saiya
Cover design: goodshepparddesign

This book is a work of nonfiction. The events and conversations in this book have been set down to the best of the author's ability, although some names and details have been changed to protect the privacy of individuals.

Visit www.thesalarymanbook.com

Dedication

For my family. Mom and Dad, you've always been there for me. And when you weren't, my mentor/tormentor Pete was there to teach all those American habits that Japan has had to wring out of me.

Siddy, you're the best. Those living room tackle football games we played growing up, using you as the football, will be in the next book.

salaryman (săl′ə-rē-măn′) *n.* 1. A Japanese businessman who works very long hours every day. 2. In Japan, a man who works in an office for a salary.

Cambridge Business English Dictionary
Cambridge University Press

Table of Contents

Preface xi

INTRODUCTION: How I became a salaryman xxi

PART I: SALARYMAN BASIC TRAINING 1

Chapter 1   The Art of the Tokyo Nap 3
To run with the salarymen, you must first learn to nap like them.

Chapter 2   Japan Wastes Not, but I Want A lot 11
Ditch those wasteful American habits and adopt Japanese "mottainai" self-discipline.

Chapter 3   A Salaryman Makeover 19
Out with my Brooks Brothers, and in with the ultra-light business clothing style that prevents the summertime salaryman "kareishuu" body odor.

Chapter 4   Cleaning Your Way Through a Japanese Day 25
Getting yellow-carded by the human resources department for having an "unrefreshing" desk and other lessons in Japanese cleanliness.

Chapter 5   Smooshed in the City 33
Learn the essential, passive-aggressive "basho tori" Japanese skill of snagging a seat or place in line in the Tokyo crowds.

Chapter 6   American Comfort Food 45
A lifelong Chicago Bulls obsession rescues me from immigrant identity loss.

Chapter 7 What Happens to the Nail that Sticks Up 53
The hammer comes down hard on Americans on the Japanese driver's license test course.

Chapter 8 Feed Your Inner Salaryman Beast 61
The key to happiness as a salaryman is constant retail indulgence.

PART II: DRINKING & OTHER SALARYMAN SKILLS 73

Chapter 9 My *Sake* Master 75
Lessons from a wise, old salaryman.

Chapter 10 Empty Stomach Boozing 101 87
The deeper side of the standard all-you-can-drink Japanese company dinners.

Chapter 11 The Foreign Guest Honey Trap 97
The charms of Japanese nighttime hospitality can be a secret negotiation weapon when foreign business partners visit Japan.

Chapter 12 The Secret Cash Stash 105
How Japanese companies help salarymen skim their paychecks for extra spending money and hide it from their wives.

Chapter 13 American Manner Buffer 115
The standard role for foreigners of shielding your Japanese bosses from rough American manners during U.S. business trips.

Chapter 14 The Gulf of Manners 121
Keeping the peace between Japanese and Korean businessmen.

PART III: SALARYMAN HEALTHCARE 127

Chapter 15   Mitamacare 129
The brutal efficiency of the Japanese universal healthcare annual examination.

Chapter 16   My Colonoscopy Vacation 137
A desperate attempt to use a colonoscopy as a socially acceptable escape from the salaryman workaholic grind.

Chapter 17   Samurai Orthopedic Surgeon 143
The before, during and after of going under the Japanese knife.

PART IV: ADVANCED TOPICS 151

Chapter 18   Reverse Culture Shock 153
Japanese toilet withdrawal, feeling like a foreigner in my home country and other aspects of my three-month transfer back to the U.S.

Chapter 19   Hello Work! 171
The many subtle humiliations of being an unemployed salaryman in Japan.

Chapter 20   The Invisible Hand of the Tokyo Economy 177
Salaryman angst is the engine behind my new economic theory.

Chapter 21   The Golden Years of Salarymanhood .. 185
The many perks of Japanese seniority.

Chapter 22   Getting Out 195
Lessons learned after nearly a decade in the salaryman trenches.

Preface

Tokyo, Shibuya—February 21, 2008, 6:25pm.

I SAT SWEATING IN A bright, stuffy meeting room on the top floor of a towering Shibuya office building. The Brooks Brothers suit I was wearing, cool and comfortable in the Southern California I always wore it, was damp and bunched up at the crotch and shoulders, and felt like a horse blanket.

The room was at least five degrees hotter than any Western male could ever take.

I had flown in to Tokyo the night before from my home in Los Angeles, and was there for a final job interview at the headquarters of one of Japan's biggest conglomerates. Preceding this had been six lumbering months of awkward, enthusiastic cross-border interviews; there'd been meetings with them in West Coast hotels, sync-ups at U.S. airport lounges and teleconference calls with them in Japan. Each interview was always followed by weeks of disturbing silence, where I imagined they were changing their minds about hiring an American like me and moving him all the way to Japan. But I'd always end up hearing back from them.

The little room I was waiting in was across a hallway from the place where my interview would happen, a standard Fortune 500-type boardroom with a perfect view of the famous neon-lit Shibuya Crossing. The trendy youth that flocked in the glowing, ultra-modern shopping area down below stood in stark contrast to the staid tradition I faced that night: three aging Japanese executives were waiting silently in the boardroom to meet me at precisely 6:30pm, and decide my fate.

If they approved, I'd move to Tokyo the next month to become one of only a handful of foreigners in their entire company of 50,000+ employees.

The whole thing suddenly seemed crazy. I, at that time a 32-year old product manager at a small LA software startup with almost zero Japanese language skills, was somehow on the brink of accepting a one to two-year contract in Tokyo as some sort of international sales manager for this company's semiconductor division. Or was it product planning they wanted me for? It was still unclear. And then after my Tokyo stint, they'd said in prior interviews, I'd be transferred as a "product director" to a new San Jose research center they were planning to open!

It all sounded cool and I went with it, after all this was one of Japan's biggest companies. Still, I had doubts. I had come all this way with them without getting any of the normal details about what my actual responsibilities would be. I let it go each time, giving in to their bureaucracy and the language gap, and not shaming them by pushing for details.

The reasons for this charade are obvious now: I was drunk on their groping, earnest courtship (despite not really being qualified for it), and they had no other candidates nor the faintest clue about how to recruit a non-Japanese. It was a classic microcosm of the exciting, flawed mutual attraction that we often see between Japanese and Americans.

I'd thought the answers to my questions would come on this trip. But my companion in the waiting room—an English-speaking veteran of the company who was my trip host—told me that this interview was really just a formality.

In the cab on the way over, he'd said that I was already hired basically, and that these interviewers didn't have any of the details I wanted to know. They just wanted to "check the look of me" and "make sure I seemed OK", before finally rubber-stamping my hire.

I remember snapping, "Jesus, so I flew from LA to Tokyo just to be looked at up and down?", while also realizing in a panic that I'd committed in spirit to a job in a foreign country without knowing some kind-of important details. Like, you know, what my job would be and where I'd live.

Add to this that my company in LA seemed to be getting wise to the fact that I might be leaving. Right before I'd left for Tokyo, they'd heaped some random extra work onto me, and it had the vibe of them wanting to see where my head was at. This only upped the ante on this Tokyo trip even more.

I remember panicking under the weight of all this in their hot Shibuya waiting room. And my host, who was in there with me, looked like he was feeling the heat too. He'd been the one who introduced me to the company—cutting through cultural barriers the size of the Pacific—through a shared connection we had in LA. Crossing the Pacific Ocean itself was no problem for us, but maybe while he saw me there – squirming in frustration – he imagined the proposed 180-degree cultural leap from California software startup to one of Japan's most traditional companies blowing up in spectacular fashion in that boardroom, with my cold feet sentencing him for life to some kind of Japanese office doghouse.

I wiped the sweat on my forehead with my sleeve and tried to break the tension by cracking, "They trying to smoke me out of here?" I remember him staring at me blankly, trying to understand the joke, right before I was called in for the interview.

As I walked into the boardroom, I remember thinking that just two days before I'd been part of an all-hands meeting at my LA company where the closing comment by a director dressed in shorts and flip-flops was, "If we get this deal, we're not just going to be rich; we're going to be '*Fuck You*' rich!"

The cultural gulf I was trapeze-ing across hit me like a truck when I saw my interviewers sitting there:

. . .

I got the job. Despite my sweat and sloppy appearance, I passed for their idea of what a foreigner at their company should look and act like. And I accepted the offer. The relief of getting through their half-year interview gauntlet – and the job's salary – ended up trumping the serious questions I had about my actual duties.

I'd learned in the first small-talk moments that the masks they were wearing were standard business gear in late February, that hapless time in Japan where it's both flu and pollen season at the same time (merit points are earned for this courtesy of wearing a mask at most Japanese offices, as it shows you're doing your best to not spread flu germs that you may or may not have). It was an early display to me of how even lofty executives in Japan religiously follow the social doctrine of what I refer to throughout this book as "Manner Mode": the impossibly high standard of courtesy, cleanliness and self-discipline that's built into everyday Japanese life (Manner Mode is actually the term used in Japan – it's pronounced *"manna-moh-dou"* – for the silent mode setting on your mobile phone, a public courtesy they promote on trains here).

The formality of that final interview foreshadowed what was to come for me in Japan. The dreamy-sounding future transfer to the new San Jose office never happened, as the 2008-9 financial crisis hit them hard and wiped out their expansion plans, and generally drained their enthusiasm for becoming more global. By year two I was no longer a short-term expat in Japan. I was a fresh-off-the-boat immigrant.

The middle-class white-collar lifestyle in Japan is what I'm writing about, and *The Salaryman* attempts to show that much of my cultural assimilation came down to learning the formalities of Japanese Manner Mode, and unlearning a lifetime of casual American behavior. This book tries to show how unnatural, frustrating and downright fun this process is – all at the same time – for your average American dude.

This was far from my expected course in life. While most of my Japanese colleagues as grade-schoolers spent their weekday nights in cram-schools getting Manner Mode pounded into them, as a kid I mostly loafed in a leafy, airy Chicago suburb as your average Bulls basketball-obsessed, late night cable TV Skinamax-watching, sometimes-studying middle-class video game addict. I learned most of my manners from an older brother who once – after a long Saturday night of Nintendo-playing (circa 1986) and binging on bowls of candy (his idea of "taking care" of 11-year-old me) – used the vacuum cleaner to clean up my vomit. He also forgot to let the dog out that night, and while I was too sick to nightcap on some naughty R-rated flicks he'd rented, I did get to taste the fruits of Japan's economic miracle at that time when our dog lifted his leg on the Nintendo:

The Nintendo, after airing out for just a day on the patio, kept on working like new! Such an awesome display of superior Japanese manufacturing no doubt left a mark on me at that age. Because *The Salaryman* is also about my natural love for Japanese goods and services that, once I became a Tokyo immigrant, jumped to an entirely different level out of necessity. The basic fact I learned is that any mentally stable salaryman relies on Retail Japan's magical recharging properties to stay sane; we foreigners out of the gate can tap into maybe 5% of the consumer enjoyment that a Japanese can. Trying to learn the remaining 95% of the local consumer culture is a very complicated business, but was key for me. As a result this book dives into important topics such as:

> To afford the constant consumption they need to stay sane, how do many Japanese salarymen hide their personal spending from their wives, and how and why do many Japanese companies secretly conspire to help them do this?
>
> Where do you get the cool, high-tech business clothes that make working 60 hours a week in those hot Japanese offices tolerable, and also help you avoid developing the Tokyo summertime "*kareisyuu*" middle-aged man odor?
>
> What's the nighttime honey trap that some Japanese companies spring on their visiting foreign business partners, which uses the charms of their hospitality to distract and then deplete their guests physically before destroying them in the negotiating room the next day?

The truth is *I've spent huge chunks of my last decade trying to figure things like this out*. This book is an anthology of hard-earned immigrant nuggets that I hope anyone – overseas adventurers, Japanese who've lived abroad, tourists in Japan, business travelers, Japan expats, or fellow salarymen-in-training – can find useful.

Finally, *The Salaryman* is a working man, consumer's take on the US-Japan culture gap. It's based on a journal I kept while slaving away inside several hardcore domestic companies. And I was able to illustrate much of my story thanks to an unlikely collaboration I struck up years ago with the professional Japanese *manga* artist Rena Saiya.

I've read books written by people who have obviously studied seriously on the culture gap subject, but that's an entirely different thing; and there are many fine books and blogs about Japanese culture out there, mostly written by people who've found a comfy niche here on the outskirts of mainstream train-commuting, office-dwelling society. Most of these fellow immigrants did the wise, sane thing; they didn't become salarymen. So this book is for the rest of us, and for anyone who's curious about what it'd be like to trade a smoggy, crawling LA freeway commute for a sliver of space between the bodies on the 7:35am train bound for Tokyo station.

Michael Howard
Tokyo, Japan
June 2019

Introduction
How I became a salaryman

MY FIRST TWO YEARS IN TOKYO were a circus, as I was constantly pinballed between a state of being charmed by Japan and being driven crazy by the bureaucracy of my old-school company. To start off with, my company's efforts to help me find an apartment in Tokyo – they had generously paid for a separate apartment-hunting trip a few weeks before I moved – went to waste when they took too long to internally approve the lease contract, despite merely being my guarantor and not paying for my rent. The night before I left my life in LA for Japan, I learned the landlord of the apartment I'd chosen had found another tenant.

So I spent my first week in Japan crammed in a company dormitory with their new college hires, and running around Tokyo looking for an apartment right after its peak springtime moving season had ended, which is like finding a French Quarter hotel room the day before Mardi Gras. I finally found a suspiciously available 1-bedroom place in a far west Tokyo suburb that I discovered – the day after I'd signed the lease – was next to a convenience store where a *yakuza* gangster had shot and killed someone the previous month. Of course a chalk-outline of a dead body next door might be taken in stride in Los Angeles—and I'd heard the *yakuza* hunt only each other, and not civilians—but it still seemed like a bad omen.

This threat was just a hiccup, though, and my faith in Japan's famous safety and the natural kindness of its people wouldn't be disappointed. I proceeded to lose my wallet on the train, my toddler's favorite stuffed animal while riding a bike and several other precious things over the next year or so, each time the lost item miraculously finding its way back to me. But everything else went about as badly as possible.

An email to my parents a few months into the job:

At the office, a cute melody plays over the office PA system at 9:00am, 12:00pm, and 1:00pm, reminding you of the start of the work day, the start of the lunch break, and the end of the lunch break, respectively... the toilets have a button where if you push it, it plays another cute melody to cover up your noises! These salarymen only take mornings or afternoons off, never a whole day, and never, ever take more than a day off at a time. They just kind of silently slip in as lunch ends so it appears as if they might have been at a customer meeting or something in the morning...I learned that my boss, the guy who championed my hiring, blabbed openly about my salary requests during our long interview process (a Japanese entering this company never negotiates) and so now the whole office knows what I make. Regular employees at Japanese companies usually have a strict age-based salary, and everyone here is a regular employee except for me. Recently, a colleague in his early 50s was at the copy machine with me, and he whispered quietly in my ear to me in English, "Michael-san, maybe you and me, same salary". I wanted to say, "But I'm on a year-to-year contract and you have lifetime employment", but I lacked the nerve. Actually, maybe I should thank God I don't have lifetime employment here.

I was supposedly part of the company's globalization movement, but that was all grandstanding. In reality, I was thrown into their salaryman rank-and-file. I got utterly lost in their inscrutable internal policies and intranet systems, all written formally in Japanese, except for the places where my foreign name jumped off the screen in a sea of Japanese names, looking as out of place as I felt:

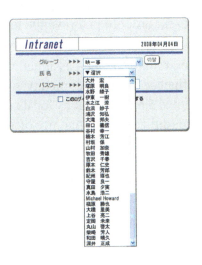

My role there was totally superfluous, and I had the presence of a souvenir left in the garage after a forgotten vacation. So I did a lot of watching, and at the end of 2008 my personal journal had the following bullet-point list of things I'd learned about this traditional Japanese company:

- If someone finds a way to save the company expenses during the year, they can't do anything about it because you're not allowed to deviate from the parent company-approved budget. Money is spent—regardless of whether the expense is needed—out of obedience to the parent company's orders.
- The hijinks are equal on the revenue side. At the end of the year used PCs and office furniture are sold by the company to another subsidiary—the company hunts for one that needs to spend the rest of its mandated expense budget—in order to pad revenue to hit the annual sales forecast.
- The only thing I've been assigned that I have any influence on is the company's so-called new global English slogans for its English website (did I mention that my official job title is "Director of Sales"?). But I wasn't given the freedom to create them from scratch myself, as a vice president of the company, known for being extremely proud of his English ability, was the de facto author. I made sure to first carefully and politely commend him on his

choices for the company's long-standing global website taglines, "Synergy for the leverage" and "The Difference is the Difference", before delicately suggesting some possible replacements.

- The employee health check for those over the age of 50 is a two-day hospital stay (everyone younger has the health check done at the office) at a company-exclusive hospital in the middle of peaceful suburban Tokyo forest where your whole body gets a complete checkup. You have your own room, and there's one nurse for every two people. It's like the executive health check at the Mayo Clinic, but free.
- The parent company deals with older executives who've grown lazy or outlived their usefulness by transferring them every two or three years to a different subsidiary. Instead of retiring them early or training them, they shovel it under the rug and give them a 20 million yen+ (~$185k) salary at each stop along with a hefty severance package when they move on.
- Just to send a customer a product sample requires our division manager's *inkan* (the traditional Japanese ink stamp used as a signature). If he's on vacation, the customer has to wait until he comes back; the respect for the manager's seniority trumps everything.
- You're limited to four times per year where you can call-in in the morning and say you aren't coming to work that same day (there's no

work-from-home policy at most Japanese companies); after that they'll ding you unpaid leave. So basically you have to predict when you, or your young kids, are going to be sick.

Of course, none of this extreme bureaucracy and executive pampering was supposed to be my long-term problem, as I was to be transferred permanently to the new San Jose office within two years. The ripples from the 2008-9 financial crisis torpedoed that plan though, as the company's revenue took a huge hit. They cancelled their plans to open up that office, stopped hiring fresh graduates and mid-career employees, and cut most of their contractors, including me after my second year.

I remember walking into our president's office for my ceremonious dismissal. He grinned sheepishly and started things off by apologizing in English, not for my being let go, but for what would be the meeting's excruciating formality: "I'm sorry…It's very Japanese style."

He then handed me a long, official dismissal statement that explained the reasons they decided not to renew my contract; they'd made both English and Japanese versions of the three-page document. He proceeded to read the whole thing to me in Japanese for five minutes without once looking up. I don't recall most of what was written, other than it said that because my project was terminated, I was no longer needed. And while my project at the company for the previous two years had been internally called "the *San*

Jose project", the statement repeatedly referred to it as the "*Saint John's* project".

It seemed like a fitting end to the job.

• • •

After I'd licked my wounds, I had to decide whether I should double-down on working in Japan, or slink back to the West Coast. Yes this first job in Japan had failed badly, but I'd enjoyed the quirks of being an immigrant in Japan. I could say only three short phrases in kindergarten-level Japanese in front of my family and friends back in the States and they'd declare "You're fluent!" before the 30-second American attention span closed and they got back to talking about the presidential election and how the Cubs needed another arm in the bullpen. And after a fun night out drinking with Japanese colleagues, I'd receive delightful emails in English with the subject line, "Beer is delicious with you". And I could listen to my toddler son proudly yelling out bilingual updates once he was done with his business in the bathroom:

These kinds of fun cross-cultural hijinks are very hard to give up.

And the language follies and "Lost in Translation" moments had made things interesting. At least a couple of times a week I'd become frozen in terror over some Japanese mistake I'd make at the office. One involved emailing in Japanese my business trip flight plans to my boss, while CCing half my team. After I'd sent the email, just to check if my grammar was 100% right, I threw it into Excite's then Japanese-English translator, which then read back:

私の出発便は来週の水曜日です。=
My departing feces is next Wednesday.

Inexplicably, the same Japanese word, "便", is used for both "flight" and "feces". So there was no resulting faux pas, just a scare caused by Excite's then-dictionary.

But then, probably due to my frustration at my poor Japanese language skills, a character I called "the Naughty English Teacher" would regularly come over me and force me to teach my eager colleagues slang such as "that's fucked up", "what the hell are you smoking?" and "I've gotta piss like a race horse".

Add to this that explosive humor could erupt spontaneously at any time in the air of daily salaryman life.

Such as one time during my quarterly presentation to our company's law firm. Instead of calling their exalted and lofty firm by its correct name, Ito Yamato, twice I called them "Ito *Yokado*", which is a low-price supermarket chain I often shopped at. The firm's president, an elder, formal and always non-expressive executive seated at the head seat of the meeting room, let out a quick, impulsive laugh at my second "Ito Yokado" mistake, which caused the whole room—people had looked around the room nervously after my first mistake—to convulse with laughter.

Then one time I got into a heated argument with a grumpy older colleague over the correct price for a discontinued, or "end-of-life" (EOL), product that we were trying to clear out. A younger colleague saw my frustration and whispered to me in English, "Don't worry Michael-san. He's EOL soon too." The same colleague another time, when I announced during our weekly team meeting that my family was expecting a second child soon, made a little hand gesture that implied fornicating and said loudly, "Ahhh....American. Must... be... so... POWERFUL!"

Then I remembered a time on a central Tokyo train on a weekend night with my toddler son, when a kind-looking, middle-aged Japanese man started to try to talk to him. He was speaking Japanese to him, trying hard to get a reaction in a crowded train, and finally succeeded to get a laugh. He then turned to me and smiled to say something. I leaned my ear toward him, and he proceeded to say in loud, halting English, "I... want... you!" After some awkward, self-conscious back-and-forth in front of suddenly curious bystanders, I finally understood that what he was really trying to say was that he envied me for having a cute boy like that.

It was an easy decision. I was having far too much fun trying to figure out how to fit in and consume in this country. Little everyday discoveries would make my heart pump with inspiration, such as learning that Japan has a popular sports drink called VAAM that contains amino acids from the larvae of giant Japanese hornets. I've had a phobia of bees and hornets since I stepped on a nest when I was seven years old and got stung 40 times, so the fact that this country could make a tasty, endurance-enhancing snack out of their terrifying, nearly two-inch long Jurassic hornets…you could say I was addicted to the consumption of Japan.

But job-wise it was a totally different story, and whether I could actually transform myself to fit into a Japanese company was an open challenge. Would I really be able to stop doing things like upsetting my company's facilities department by leaving "messy-looking" toilet paper in the bathroom stall? (I had a habit of tearing the toilet paper in a rough way that left its edge angled diagonally and jigjagged, causing them to email my boss once, begging that I be more considerate of my co-workers and tear it more neatly). Las Vegas odds were against me. Pulling this kind of assimilation off would be one of the biggest upsets to happen in Japan since Buster Douglas knocked out Mike Tyson at the Tokyo Dome in 1990, but I was up for giving it the old college try. And I realized I'd barely touched the delicious salaryman perks to be had. So I stayed in Tokyo and bounced around a few different Japanese companies over the next eight years, and dedicated myself to learning the ways of a true salaryman.

PART I
SALARYMAN BASIC TRAINING

1

The Art of the Tokyo Nap

MY APARTMENT, WEST TOKYO, a little before 6:00am on a weekday in April 2008, just weeks after I'd moved to Japan. Cocooned deep inside my blankets, I'm beginning to hear the early morning sounds of Tokyo reverberate through my window. Barely dawn, it quickly builds into a steady chorus: business shoes hitting pavement, city crows cawing, truck engines starting, trash bins rattling. The noise, amplified by the packed-together apartment buildings on my street, starts to penetrate deep into my cocoon. Soon I'm awake, well before my alarm. I was already exhausted as I started that day, one of my first ever as a salaryman.

I sketch this scene because it's part of how overcrowding here feeds sleep deprivation. Every Tokyo salaryman faces this morning sleep deficit daily, and equalizes it throughout his day with a natural napping superpower.

I quickly learned that my first step to adopting Manner Mode and the salaryman lifestyle would be learning the mysterious art of the Tokyo nap. Ignoring this first step would've given me a will-sapping sleep deficit compared to my Japanese colleagues, and crippled all of my other efforts at cultural immersion that appear in this book.

A walk around Tokyo will quickly reveal that its salaryman, like an exhausted soldier in a battlefield trench, can summon at-will a quick, powerful nap even in unbearably cramped conditions. You watch in amazement when you first get here as the city is full of salarymen napping full-out in seemingly un-nappable places: in saunas, peacefully snoring away on the floor of a nursery school playroom, or even napping STANDING UP WHILE WAITING IN LINE TO NAP on a building lobby chair:

I've learned that this native napping talent blossoms out of necessity during evening cram school marathons in grammar school, and it fully matures upon entering the trenches of a Japanese company after college. It remains a flourishing life force throughout a salaryman career thanks to a perfect storm of napping conditions: the enormous energy needed to keep up Japanese manners, a predator-free environment that makes napping perfectly safe, and the sleep deprivation that comes with the salaryman lifestyle.

But we Americans are naturally too paranoid of being robbed or maimed while napping, and utterly lack this napping skill. The reality I had to learn is that the world in Japan is benign, and it takes your American instincts time to realize that and disarm themselves. There's no need to waste energy worrying about your physical safety; all of it needs to go towards summoning the patience and discipline needed for Manner Mode. Of course I hadn't figured any of this out when I first got here, and it left me as a sitting, sleep-deprived duck in the Tokyo trenches as I worked hard on my napping craft.

For months I had to take bullets and watch closely.

First, on a jammed morning train I remember marveling at an important-looking older salaryman who not only slept standing up on my train each morning, but did so deeply enough that he snored. Then, against all Western logic, I'd watch salarymen nod-off in their seats and peacefully lean their heads on the shoulder of women sitting next to them–perfect strangers!

I'd think of New York or Chicago, and how there this might lead to you getting maced, arrested, robbed, or worse. And then I'd get off the train in awe of such harmony amidst mass crowding, and start to realize that Tokyo is a kind of urban Neverland.

You must first realize that there's a great unwritten code at work here that allows citizens to nap unbothered and safe, whenever and wherever. But still, as an American, you're only used to seeing homeless people doing this and are too self-conscious to join in. So you must keep observing for a while.

Another day, I visited a Japanese customer and gave an important presentation to their top boss. During the Q&A part of my presentation I watched him—in the middle of an intense discussion that he'd started—suddenly doze off in his chair for 10 minutes.

It went almost unnoticed by the others, but afterwards I raised my natural American concern about this: that this meant that he didn't care for the presentation or was unhappy about something. My Japanese colleague waved me off with a laugh: "*Daijobu desu.* In Japan, it means that the boss is happy and has no problems. It means he's relaxed."

The lesson here was that once you're relaxed, the undercurrent of Tokyo commuting exhaustion can spontaneously take over at any time and trump any business at hand. Salarymen share this understanding with each other, and that's why they look the other way when the in-meeting ZZZs start.

And it's not just your customers who have a license to nap during meetings. Merely a few weeks inside my new Japanese office also taught me the internal use of napping: as a tool to make it through pointless meetings. Most Japanese offices love the ritual of meetings (having a meeting in order to decide the time of another meeting was a personal favorite), but even in more modern companies, rarely does anyone ever say, if a scheduled one-hour meeting's agenda is finished in 30 minutes, "OK, we're done, I'll give everyone back 30 minutes". The native style, and appropriate manner—to give the appearance that you're doing the job you set out to do in the meeting, because if some bad result later happens, a shortened meeting could be pointed to as the reason why—is that if the meeting was scheduled for an hour, then you must put in one hour, and fill those last 30 minutes with a creative mix of side-related business conversation. Ceremoniously using the meeting's entire slotted time—time that could be spent doing something far more personally productive—is the norm, with some attendees giving in to nature and being allowed to nap away.

A few months after moving to Japan I went on my first business trip to the US, and it quickly revealed the napping culture gap I was stuck in. My jet-lagged boss, after a long day of customer meetings and a few beers in a San Jose bar, fell asleep in our booth. Several customers elbowed each other to stare at the passed-out drunk Japanese guy, and the waitress anxiously asked me, "Is he OK?" I remember being mystified at all the attention, confused maybe about which side of the napping culture I was now part of, and loudly remarking, "So what? He's not drunk. He's just resting!"

Back in Japan after this, I soon found that after lunches my body would often demand I join in on the napping party. Still completely unable to nap in public, I desperately looked for a more American solution. I searched for, and happily found, a sofa in my company's basement storage room. The privacy, fresh blankets and pillows on it were enticing, but it sounded a vague alarm: my co-workers at this time slept in their chairs with their heads on their desks, but this just sits here unused?

I then dove onto it, and woke up feeling like a new man. But a feeling of overindulgence hung over me for the rest of the day. After lunch the next day, I eagerly returned to my new permanent nap spot and...instantly found it in ruins. Taped to the pillow was a sign, written in English, reading:

> Here sofa no for you.
> Only menstruate woman.
> Please thank you –
> Facility manager

This is how I learned that couches in private areas in Japanese offices are reserved for women having their monthly menstrual cycles. The facilities manager had caught me napping there the day before, and instead of waking me up, decided on this non-confrontational approach to nipping my napping bud.

I cowered back to my desk and realized there was no choice but to adopt the communal, head-on-your-desk, lunchtime salaryman napping style:

THE SALARYMAN

For weeks, I tried this in vain. I still wasn't comfortable napping in public.

Exhausted on the train home one night, I remembered George Orwell's *Down and Out in Paris and London*. Like he'd experienced as an overworked immigrant dishwasher in 1930s Paris, sleep had become a consumptive act for me and no longer just a physical need.

And then, after months of napping apprenticeship, something wonderful happened to ease my commuting salaryman pain, as so often has happened in Tokyo ever since I moved here. On the train ride home, with my American instincts weakened, I dozed off in my seat with native Japanese form. Then I magically woke up the moment my train station was announced.

And that's the moment I learned the art of the Tokyo nap.

2

Japan Wastes Not, but I Want A lot

WITH JAPANESE NAPPING TALENTS in your toolbox, you have the energy needed to transform yourself into a well-mannered salaryman. And the first thing you must do with this is absorb the concept of *mottainai* (pronounced "mo-tie-na-ee"), an absolute pillar of Japanese life.

It literally means "don't waste!" or "how wasteful!", but it's also meant to convey the deep modesty and resource conservatism that is the quintessentially earnest Japanese mindset. It's about as intuitive to us Supersize Me-minded Americans as eating pizza with chopsticks.

Sure, saying *mottainai*! has its banal, everyday uses – like getting kids to finish their dinners – but it's the guilt it injects into your everyday American habits that makes it so painful to adopt into your mannerisms. It's like a self-disciplining doctrine for Japanese manners, and it turns untrained immigrants like me into natural sinners that must repent, or be expelled from everyday Japanese society.

For me, the first thing to get *mottainai-ed* out of me here was my glorious, beloved 10-minute mid-winter hot shower, an American birthright in my native Chicago:

(And in my home: toys such as my daughter's kitchen set are programmed to sing out *"Mottainai yo!"* if any of the toy's appliances, such as the faucet, are left on too long).

Mottainai starts to put the squeeze on you from the very start of your typical salaryman day. First, I'd wake on a freezing winter morning. Not in a centrally heated bedroom like in the U.S., but in my space-heated tatami room that's turned into a meat locker overnight. I begin the winter day with this ecological good deed—sleeping in a meat locker instead of wasting electricity on heating—but then must deal with the morning *mottanai* hangover: your body undergoes a brutal internal thawing as you creak into the kitchen for breakfast, like a Sci-Fi space traveler emerging from hypersleep.

I'd think of my beloved American-portioned hot shower to thaw out. But taking showers in the morning is not the norm for salarymen: most see it as a waste of water, and a pain to clean up (because of the humid climate, you MUST wipe every surface of your shower dry after each use to prevent mold from growing, or so I'm told). So instead, to warm up, I heat up the remaining *nabe* broth from last night's dinner and toss in leftover rice to create a nice breakfast stew, soaking up every last ounce of broth. I try to use my foreign, amateur chopstick skills to nab every last grain of rice in my bowl, enacting a lesson pounded into every Japanese child: the meal's not over until every last tiny grain is gone.

All this *mottainai* nitpicking is dreadful so early in the morning, especially without a hot shower to wake up (that goes double if you're suffering from a hangover from the standard Japanese office nocturnal drinking). *Mottainai* even prevents you from taking care of your morning bathroom business in your customary way: using the standard American man-wipe amount of toilet paper was banned in my home after I once caused a major toilet overflow disaster:

The pipes under my house, in typical Tokyo fashion, the plumber lectured me, were very winding and narrow due to lack of space, so I was ordered from then on to use two or three toilet paper squares per wipe at most, which took great concentration to execute for a typical clumsy American like me.

After my careful morning trip to the bathroom, I'd grab my company-paid train pass, reminding myself that it can only be used on the lowest-fare route to the office. So I couldn't add some variation or a more scenic route to my monotonous 90 minute commute, unless I wanted to pay my own way. My deflationary salaryman paycheck made this an unlikely *mottainai* choice, sentencing me to the same, unvarying robotic daily commute. My payoff from this boredom was my recent mastery of napping on packed trains. And I found that this infusion of badly needed sleep would propel me to face *mottainai* the rest of my day.

During my weekly cleaning duty at my office that morning—little money is spent on professional cleaning at most offices because Japanese employees all possess *mottainai* manners—I managed to wipe the office furnishings clean without bitching about it, thanks to my nap.

Then, in an afternoon meeting, there was a discussion about ways to spend the remaining annual budget that the parent company had allocated for exhibitions and events for that year, featuring plans to promote a long-time underperforming product. I openly questioned the return on investment of spending time and budget on minor events, and why the company continued to fund a known dud of a product. Because, it was explained to me, the parent company's management went to the trouble to formally approve this large budget, and millions of dollars were already sunk into the product's development. It'd be too shamefully *mottainai* to waste this blessed budget and these sunk costs.

In one fell swoop, and on both counts, *mottainai*-guilt trumped standard business school logic.

Then, on many days during my idle time, I'd look over from my desk in the overseas sales department at the domestic Japanese salespeople, and watch in awe of what they were doing as they talked on the phone with their customers. They'd be making little servile head-bows into the phone as they talked to them in perfect Japanese *keigo* (vocabulary using extra-polite honorifics and grammar), and then they'd end each call not by casually throwing the phone down with a small thud as an American would, but by gently laying the handset back down silently as if they were putting a newborn baby down to sleep.

From where did they summon this effort to be so overly polite *even when nobody could see it and appreciate it?* Or more bluntly, I asked further, *what's the point of bowing to someone who can't see you?* I was told by one colleague: "because of *mottainai*". This is one of my pocket theories on Japan that should be taken with a grain of salt, but a quick Wikipedia check later confirmed something: the concept of *mottainai* is some kind of mix of Buddhist frugality and the Japanese Shinto respect for the souls living within man-made objects. If there's any truth to that, then man, how's that for a melting pot? But unlike the US melting pot tendency to Panda-Express cultural nuance into a melded and chewy American nugget, the Japanese melting pot seems to work in the opposite way. It spits out hard-core ideals like *mottainai*; sharp and refined as a samurai sword.

Halfway through the train ride home at night, most of us salarymen would go for a little liquid escape from all the *mottainai* pressure. But after being so monastic all day, a few sips is really all you need. So at the station kiosk I'd often spring for the tiny, TSA-compliant sized-looking can of beer they sell, rather than going for the normal 12 oz. can:

Then I'd stop in my neighborhood tofu shop and pick up a six-pack of doughnuts that they make out of the leftover slivers of tofu that pile up throughout the day in the vats.

I'd finally get home and immediately join my toddler in the bath. This is the period each day I was bound to hear a crack about my American overindulgence with hot water in the shower.

When we were done bathing I wouldn't drain the tub, as this would be considered wasteful of the water. Instead, I set my clothes washer to "bathwater" mode and connected a tube from the washer to the inside of the bathtub. Pumping in the used (but still clean) bathwater to the clothes washer saved us from wasting new water and would be – at last! – my final *mottainai* move of the day:

Almost ready for bed, I'd say the hell with all this conservation, and pop open a big 16 oz. Asahi brewski. And as I'd guzzle it, I'd glance over at my kid's little toy kitchen, waiting for it to scold me with "*Mottainai*!!"

3

A Salaryman Makeover

AFTER MASTERING NAPPING and *mottainai* manners, one of the first of your next assimilations is to learn how to dress in order to survive the steamy Tokyo summer train commute. The seasonal side effects of broiling yourself on the summer trains are numerous. First, there's the resulting "summer fatigue" sickness known as *natsubate* that inevitably strikes the Japanese salaryman down. It's a form of mild heat exhaustion that hits each victim differently, and it usually attacked me in a jammed rush-hour train in the form of, let's just say, an urgent need to find a toilet.

On Tokyo summer morning train commutes, you'll occasionally see a salaryman frantically plow his way off the train—one of the few displays of roughness in a crowd you'll ever see here—to get to a bathroom. This is a dangerous game to play in the world's most crowded city, and I learned that you need to have in your head a mental checklist of the best, most reliably available public toilets near each station along your train commute.

[Side note: Train bathrooms should NOT be on a foreigner's toilet GPS, as they're filled with Japanese-style toilets—basically porcelain holes in the ground—

which require the flexibility and balance of an Olympic gymnast in order to avoid creating a scatological crime scene.]

Everybody's personal anecdote to *natsubate* is different, and Tokyo gives you infinite retail options to heal yourself physically or mentally. My *natsubate* elixir was simply the bowel-settling peace of mind that my mental Tokyo toilet map gave me (a big *arigato!* to the Subway sandwich shop at my train transfer point, Meidaimai station – wonderful facilities!).

Then there's the nasty "middle-aged man smell" summer condition known as *kareishuu* that secretes from the sweating, hungover, *sake*-reeking heads (not the armpits, but HEADS!) of consumptive salarymen on the packed trains. *Kareishuu* is a sign of summertime starting in Tokyo—like *edamame* coming into season—and its stench can knock many a train commuter off their stride:

Thankfully, the Japanese clothing industry has honed-in on the *kareishuu* problem, and unleashed otherworldly Japanese textile technology on it in the form of "Cool Biz" clothing, a type of ultra-breathable casual business clothes that you can find in most salaryman clothing stores.

Cool Biz stems from a Japanese government energy-saving mandate that urges Japanese offices to set their air-conditioning no lower than the balmy, *kareishuu*-inducing temperature of 27 degrees Celsius (82.4 Fahrenheit) during summer. Japanese companies here have so dutifully followed this (thanks to *mottainai* duty) that clothing manufacturers have found themselves basking in a ready-made *kareishuu*-prevention business.

Early on, I realized that I, middle-aged guy myself, was in danger of blossoming into a *kareishuu* man if I didn't quickly adopt Cool Biz clothes into my wardrobe. You see, low-tech cottony American business clothes simply don't cut it in the merciless Japanese summer heat. Once you remove the ample air-conditioning, car commuting and roomy, cool offices and homes of the U.S, this becomes obvious.

Removed of these lazy American comforts, your Tokyo world becomes a steamy blur of concrete and train cars, with waves of commuters flowing around you in tight spaces. The first month of this 35 C–plus degree heat—with the 27 C-plus-degree Japanese office—not only melted five quick pounds off my lazy American car-commuter frame, but it also blatantly exposed my business wardrobe as being totally unfit for the heat of a Tokyo summer.

The heat, trains and walking soon ground-away at the shabby and ill-fitting parts of my American male wardrobe. What's par for the course in white-collar America looks sloppy in the sea of comfortable Tokyo salarymen dressed in Cool Biz. I'd marvel at how after getting tossed and turned in hellishly hot and packed morning trains, these salarymen would fall out of the train car without a hair out of place, while I'd emerge looking like Saddam Hussain did after two weeks of hiding in an Iraqi bunker.

It all came to a head for me one summer morning during my first year here. I was walking to work with a horde of other commuters when I noticed a limp-looking, disheveled white man – possibly a homeless person – walking toward me. With a shock, I realized it was my own image reflected in a building window:

I was sweat-soaked with a drenched shirt that was willfully untucked on the sides. My hair was disheveled, my face was flushed and my cotton pants were bunched up at the crotch. At that moment, I knew my accustomed, American bland-and-boxy, cotton-and-starch American Brooks Brothers-style would never survive Tokyo.

Cool Biz clothing would be my savior. It literally feels like wearing a swimsuit to work compared to US business clothes, using extremely thin, lightweight, water-absorbing advanced textile materials developed in Japan *for Japanese men.*

That last part is key, as it implies a certain middle-aged body slimness, and results in a tightness-of-fit that gives the average middle-aged American dude pause. First, the Cool Biz socks have this brilliant Japanese "stay-up technology" which seems like a godsend to those of us who've been driven crazy their whole lives by loose American business socks that fall down your calves. But I found them so effective that they left a ridiculous, stapled-looking sock-line on my calves that would, after the workweek ended, stay solidly imprinted through summer weekends when I was always wearing shorts.

And add to this that the ultra-smooth, tight, thin material of Cool Biz business pants felt almost too... ahem... *delightful* down there around my groin area.

So while Cool Biz clothing created a very real risk of me being deported for having an unruly erection on the crowded morning train, it did allow me to work like a demon with my Japanese colleagues through even the hottest of mid-summer Tokyo heat waves. And I managed to keep *kareisyuu* at bay. And for me, that was a good trade.

4

Cleaning Your Way Through a Japanese Day

THE PRESSURE TO BE SUPER-CLEAN AND NEAT is on you from the very start of your day in Japan. You fling open your bathroom door first thing in the morning, and it triggers the toilet's motion-triggered auto-cleaning function, a standard feature of toilets here.

Its sidelights flip on and the unit makes a sizzling, internal spraying sound as it automatically cleans and moistens the sides of the bowl in preparation for your arrival:

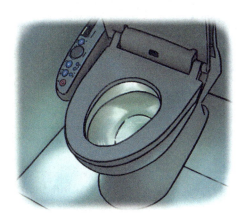

The morning toilet self-cleaning sets the tone for the rest of a typical day, which would often proceed as follows.

I hurry to separate my burnable from my non-burnable garbage, as in Japan you have to somehow fit all your burnable garbage into one tiny trash can that looks presentable to the neighborhood. This takes most of my time, and I wave good-bye in a rush to my son sitting down to his cereal as I head out the door:

I want to stay and clean it up, but there's no time for that, much less eating any cereal. I have to catch my train to work, as there's no flex-time at most Japanese companies.

I arrive at the office and do a double take at the outside entrance. My boss, a lofty vice president, is sweeping the area with a broom and dust collector and wearing white work gloves, the whole bit. I then remember that in egalitarian Japan, everyone from top to bottom at the company shares cleaning duties on a rotating basis.

I go into the men's room after I arrive in the office, and see three middle-aged Japanese men standing in front of the sinks with their heads tilted towards the ceiling in exactly the same manner, gargling water grotesquely and then spitting it out. Standard Tokyo office hygiene after an hour spent commuting in a packed train car full of people coughing and sniffling.

After that, I finally get to my desk, hungry and already tired of all this cleanliness. I take another gut-punch when the first thing that greets me is a little yellow warning card put on my desk by HR. Its nagging instructions say you must clean off your desk COMPLETELY before leaving the office every night:

**Yellow card translated:
"make the desktop refreshingly clean, OK?"**

This nearly sets me off, but I decide I better just eat something and settle down. But you have no privacy at your desk in this country—there are no cubicles in your typical Japanese office, just row-upon-row of desks thrown on top of each other. You're like baseball players sitting side-by-side in a dugout. I chuckle when realizing that if I spun around 360 degrees while sitting in my chair with my arms spread-eagled, I'd clip the two people sitting next to me and barely miss the one in front. This communal atmosphere makes eating at your desk a no-no.

Despite this, I then quietly dig out a little bag of Doritos from my drawer, give a peek left and right to make sure the coast is clear, and wolf the whole bag in 10 seconds. My hunger is satisfied, but I now have orange Dorito-fingers. I start to look for the little moist toilettes I'm sure I had in my drawer—the damn things are everywhere in Japan and now, after eating Doritos of course, I can't find one!

Suddenly, from my left, I'm greeted in formal Japanese with, "*Sumimasen,* Michael-san! Nice to meet you..." I jump up, and my eyes widen as I see it's the company CEO, a very formal Japanese executive, making an unannounced visit to my desk. Everyone in the office stops what they're doing to watch our exchange as he still hasn't met me, the only foreigner in the company, yet. I must make a good impression, so I stiffen my posture and clasp my Dorito hands behind my back in a nice, humble-looking Japanese pose. He then, as I hoped he would not, puts his hand out for a Western-style handshake, and after doing a panicky hand wipe on my back pant leg, I shake it. As he walks away, I assume that he now thinks all Americans must work with dirty Dorito hands at their desk in the morning.

Next, during the most frantic part of my day—getting my next overseas business trip approved by my boss—it's announced everyone must put on a medical mask as one of our colleagues went home with the flu that day. Office rules in Japan dictate that a colleague getting the flu means you all must act as if you've just entered an Ebola hot zone in order to prevent spreading the flu germs flying around the office.

My boss soon starts to bark at me about my trip schedule, but his face is covered with a mask and it muffles his voice. Not being able to see his lips move throws off my Japanese comprehension. In frustration, he gets in my face and shouts *"hii ga chigau!"* ("the days are wrong!"). But, what I think I hear is *"hiya ke daro!"* ("your face is sunburned!"):

I fumble with the exchange for a few minutes and finally fall back into my desk in a funk, all caused by this fanatical cleanliness. The final body-blow comes as I'm about to leave the office and all this nitpicking behind for the day. As a follow-up to the morning yellow card, an HR lackey arrives to hand me the following helpful guide to properly cleaning my desk before going home each night:

"O" is for yes, do it this way, "X" is for unacceptable

And then he stays to watch me clean it.

But that's not quite the end yet. As a salaryman, your nightly hot bath waiting for you at home is one of your precious few chances at relaxing during the week. But it's more complicated for a hairy-chested foreigner like me. (and that's understating it. I'm a proud member of the Tom Selleck Hairy Chest All-Star Team).

You see, families share the same bathwater at night in Japan. It's much cleaner than it sounds as everyone washes themselves before getting in. Adding to the Japanese assumption of perfect cleanliness is that Japanese guys are evolutionarily designed to be smooth and hairless, like seals, for perfect, non-hair-shedding bathing.

This built-in cleanliness is very family-friendly, as it leaves no floating hairs in the bath. So Japanese dads surely have never been, as I have repeatedly, on the receiving end of a "Hair! *Kitanai* (dirty)!" complaint echoing through the bathroom:

To complete my adoption of Japanese-level cleanliness, I may have to just break out the Nair and razor and, with Diane Ross' *"I'm Coming Out"* playing in the background, have myself a shaving party.

5
Smooshed in the City

NAPPING, DRESSING AND CLEANING in the salaryman style prepares you to live, commute, bathe, drink and work with the horde of 11,000 people existing in your average, everyday, overcrowded Tokyo square mile (twice the density of L.A. and New York). Tokyo salaryman life literally becomes a constant effort of maintaining Manner Mode while you politely fight for your own personal space or place in line in super-crowded places like commuter trains, restaurants with limited seating and events with long lines.

This delicate dance is called *basho tori* ("taking a spot"), and like napping in public and *mottainai*, it's an essential life skill that immigrants must acquire here. Without this skill, you'll be constantly 10 steps behind your fellow Japanese whenever you go out in public and try to do anything.

The *basho tori* instinct is a core part of being a Tokyo Japanese, and using it is invisibly weaved into every kind of daily life situation imaginable. For instance, after the great Eastern Japan earthquake and nuclear disaster in 2011, there was a nationwide panic over the radioactivity of domestic vegetables. At supermarkets, the panic was palpable, especially when veggies from so-called safe areas would go on sale. Not knowing how to politely *basho tori* my way through a dozen old ladies (I'd gotten there first!) and into these veggie sale baskets—and having to go home with lettuce and mushrooms that may have glowed in the dark—was my first exposure to how vital this skill is.

Or another example, every October kindergartens and grade schools in Japan have a big Saturday athletic meet (called the *"Undou Kai"*) where the kids play orchestrated games, run relay races, do group dances, etc., in front of throngs of parents watching it all through a camera lens. Pretty much standard issue stuff you see in most countries.

But because of an innate awareness of the lack of space on these school grounds (and add a dash of the famous photo-taking mania of the Japanese), there's an intense competition by Japanese dads to grab the best seats on the school grounds so they can get the best close-up photos of their kids in action.

The most motivated dads camp out *all night* in front of the school—like you see people do for rock concert tickets in other countries—in order to be first through the gates in the early morning to claim the best seats, which they do by throwing down their picnic seat cover on a plot of the seating area, thereby "claiming" a spot on the ground (there's no seating).

I'd learn this *basho tori* lesson the hard way.

I'd been gently warned beforehand that seat claiming was competitive, so for my son's first kindergarten *Undou Kai*, I arrived with my own picnic cover at

7:00am, two hours ahead of the 9:00am event. On the way there on my bike I applauded myself, thinking of what a good Tokyo salaryman dad I was by doing this so early on a Saturday morning.

But that fantasy vanished when I got there and saw a line of at least 100 other dads already there in line. Those at the front had been there for hours and were relaxing with portable chairs, coolers, books and newspapers. My frustration at this passive-aggressive competiveness led me to kid the other dads around me, and I asked if the etiquette after we all got into the school ground was to run all out and elbow each other out of the way. They all scoffed at the idea of such uncivil behavior in Japan, and gave me a "No, no, no. Never. Of course not!"

Then the instant the school gates opened, it was as if a starting gun went off. The innate, competitive Tokyo *basho tori* impulse suddenly overtook them, and these well-mannered salarymen dads suddenly turned into settlers from the Oklahoma Land Rush of 1889, stampeding past me with their picnic covers in hand:

And so it was that I had to settle for a seat of my kids events from a back row spot looking over several rows of earlier risers. As I stewed over the bad view from my bad seat, a guy in the section behind me calmly improved his view with a brilliant little stool:

I made a mental note: the Japanese seem to have a little *basho tori* prop or skill to deal with any overcrowding problem.

(Side note: And nursery schools for toddlers are so overcrowded in Tokyo that I'd have to speed-dial the school dozens of times at the designated "sign-up" time every month to get appointments for my toddler son at the time. Hundreds of households in our area at the same time were pounding their phones too in a *basho tori* attempt to get through the line's busy signal and snag an appointment).

Then there's the morning commuter trains, where *basho tori* is elevated to an art form. Everyone's seen the images of the super-crowded Tokyo commuter trains. Inside these bogs of irritation grind you to a pulp during the summer, especially when you add things like…

> the hangover from the previous night's required company drinking party, or…
>
> the leg itch or drop of sweat hanging off your nose that you can't get to with your pinned arms, or…
>
> the steaming body of the salaryman tangled up with you that reeks of last night's *sake* and garlic *gyoza*, or…
>
> your wrap-style earphone cable snagging on somebody's briefcase, almost lynching you by your ear like this…

I've managed to isolate the culprit of this situation: the no flex time/work-at-home policy of Japanese companies. Since an individualistic perk like this is rare in group-fixated Japanese companies, 30 million Tokyo souls must all live within 90 minutes of the central city and hit the commuter trains during the same two-hour window. This drives normally reserved 90 pound women, desperately trying to make it to work on time, to brutishly *basho tori* their way into overflowing trains. The local technique for this back-in move into the scrum on the morning train is the same way a post player in basketball backs their defender down toward the hoop with their butt:

But just as with the man with the stool proved at the *Undou Kai*, there's always a brilliant little elixir here to balance out the uncomfortable lack of space. In the case of crowded trains, there's that natural Japanese ability to nap on demand, even standing up. And add to this the public license to carelessly crack open a beer, anywhere you please, even on a packed train.

It's during these beer-sipping train moments that I want to raise my can to salute Tokyo. If only it gave me the elbowroom to do so.

• • •

Then there's Tokyo Disneyland, which takes *basho tori* to magical levels. One time I got a personal taste of it. I was there for my son's birthday, and we hit the park running at 10am on a perfect 26-degree weekday. We barely missed one Tokyo twist on the Disneyland experience: the daily, polite stampede when the gates open at 9am, where tens of thousands of people burst inside to snatch "Fastpass" reservation tickets for the most popular rides (a New York Times article once compared it to Spain's Running of the Bulls, saying it's the only Disney theme park in the world exhibiting such behavior).

This burst of *basho tori* would be background to our little family saga later that day. You see, there's a flip side to *basho tori*: the innate skill of navigating, surviving and even enjoying yourself in a Tokyo crowd, all while maintaining a Japanese-standard of manners.

It sounds simple, but it's not. To be a Tokyo citizen is to be a master of the public sidestepping, nod-giving and arm-tucking that allows you to actually get places and secure your space while not bowling people over, falling onto train tracks or generally having a Godzilla-like effect on the country. Japanese learn this skill by osmosis from a young age, but foreigners like me and very young kids like my son are fledgling *basho tori*-ers. We're a high-risk minority in a Japanese crowd.

Nobody knows all this better than Tokyo Disneyland.

At about 5pm we were going strong and having a bathroom break in the Fantasyland area. My son and I were waiting for his friend, who was in the bathroom, in front of a little Pinocchio-themed fountain. A huge, neon parade of Disney floats was moving by right in front of us. A huge crowd was blocking his view, so my son stepped up on the fountain edge and started skitting around all the people that were sitting on it.

His *basho tori* lane-change quickly veered into a ditch.

I remember telling him to be careful, and then looked away for just long enough. In one of those moments every parent has had, I turned back to see him, seemingly in slow motion, lose his balance and flop into the fountain. Horrified, I yanked him out. He was unhurt, but completely soaked from head to toe and screaming bloody murder for what seemed like an eternity. I tried and failed to calm him down in front of probably about 300 onlookers:

I sensed a ruined birthday, a ruined Disney experience and a long car ride home. But little did I know that my son's accident had sounded a very special kind of silent alarm. A masterful situation-fixing mechanism began to work inside the walls of Tokyo Disneyland. You could call it a magic wand with a spell-blend of Disney service and Japanese *basho tori*.

I kneeled in a cloud of panic and embarrassment in front of my screaming son, and remember at first some Disney attendants rushing to us with towels. And then—and here is where my shame and confusion make my memory hazy—a wave of secondary help spontaneously appeared in the form of several middle-aged Japanese ladies, all looking like your normal Disneyland guest.

They first helped me calm and dry-off my son. Then these ladies unleashed an otherworldly spell on us: *within three minutes* they'd stocked my son with used-but-immaculate, and somehow *perfect-fitting,* pants, underwear, socks and t-shirt. As quickly as they'd appeared, these ladies vanished before I could gather my wits and do the thanking and phone number-writing I felt obliged to do.

Now there are plenty of countries where you'll get a nice Good Samaritan story out of a small disaster like this. But the whole understated efficiency of what had happened here spelled out *elite Japanese Disney operation.* We got whisked to the Fantasyland first-aid room, and within 30 minutes my son emerged bone-dry (even his shoes!). He was none the worse for all this and even seemed to have an extra skip in his step all the way until closing time.

I strongly suspect now that what we'd experienced was the magic of the plain-dressed army of Tokyo Disneyland "*basho tori* accident" professionals that Tokyo Disneyland is rumored to employ. They apparently float around the park all day, quietly snuffing out minor guest discomforts and little *basho-tori* accidents like ours with their fairy dust. That they look like regular visitors is no accident. It only adds to the extra-level of Disney-enchanted Manner Mode you feel at Tokyo Disneyland.

6

American Comfort Food

HOW MUCH CAN YOU bend and contort yourself to fit into a totally different culture until you start to lose your mind? A few years into learning Manner Mode, you start to feel it sand away at the core of your American identity. For me, this created not only an identity crisis, but also an even more serious void of boredom that needed to be filled somehow, especially since I hadn't yet mastered the ways of true salaryman consumption. A small but important part of my answer to this crisis was creating – sadly enough – my own little virtual country club to escape to, one centered around my lifelong obsession with the Chicago Bulls.

I've used the Bulls my whole life to deal with life whenever it gets too heavy and formal. Whether it's an American church event or college graduation ceremony, or a typical day as a foreigner at a Japanese company, my personal space-creating, responsibility-avoiding, small rebellion-making, step-back three-point shot has always been sneaking away to watch a Bulls game.

I've read many times that sports team obsessions can retard male emotional growth. That it blocks us from relating to our kids and our significant others, and generally creates an excuse for all sorts of childish behavior. So I'm proud that I've added a legitimate immigration-related reason to the short list supporting middle-aged men with kids being allowed to obsess over a sports team (certainly my chosen team's performance over the past decade is not on this list).

But life for an obsessive NBA fan in Tokyo is complicated. Tip-off is always sometime mid-morning. Because of this time difference I often have to shut down my daytime social media completely and limit personal email to friends who aren't basketball fans and are unlikely to be spoilers.

Sometimes when there's an important game going on the distraction is too much to handle at the Tokyo office. I'll squirm until I find a way to watch at least the fourth quarter live on my smartphone in some dark, semi-private office corner. This is when I add to my un-proud legacy of playing hooky to watch the Bulls.

Below I own-up to the top five Bulls hooky moments in my life, now featuring some entries done in a desperate escape from my salaryman drudgery:

5. Sunday, May 17, 1992: Bulls vs. New York Knicks, Eastern Conference Semi-Finals, Game 7

The Bulls were an ascending championship dynasty with Michael Jordan at his peak, and the Knicks had them on the ropes in round two with their pounding, brutish play. The Bulls *became* a dynasty by winning this game, and my obsession was at its adolescent peak. I was 17 and flew in from Chicago to suburban L.A. with my family the day before for my older brother's college graduation. The pomp and circumstance, my brother's accomplishments, the family pride, the pretty college girls, the lure of sunny California college life—these incredible life forces couldn't stop me from bailing on the ceremonies to go find a TV in the empty dorms.

There was really no resisting it. A classic Game 7 against a hated enemy, Jordan's brilliance, and my Bulls love at its apex. I got lit into by my parents after this one – my brother too was livid, not at me of course but at missing Jordan score 42 to slay the Knicks – and it marked the first time guilt entered the picture for my Bulls hooky habit. This all foreshadowed a more complicated adult future.

Footnote: I believe, in some subconscious attempt to make up for this, I actually let my high school prom date the following spring convince me to not watch Game 3 of the Bulls-Phoenix Suns Finals game on Sunday, June 13, 1993. Instead, I properly joined her for a day-after-prom late lunch with our party-mates at some stupid Cracker Barrel restaurant. And yes, I blamed her for the Bulls' brutal triple overtime loss that day.

4. Saturday, May 24, 1997, Bulls vs. Miami Heat, Eastern Conference Finals, Game 3

Flash forward five years, and I replayed the same act AT MY OWN GRADUATION FROM THE SAME COLLEGE. Only this time, there was really no reason for the urgency and I should've been acting five years more mature, and I would've if I'd had a girlfriend at the time. The Bulls were up 2-0 in the series and in full dynasty mode against an inferior opponent. The NBA TV schedule was a little more favorable, and I managed to arrive, to knowing looks from my friends, by the end of the commencement speech (given by Steven Forbes no less).

Nick Hornby, the famous obsessive Arsenal soccer fan, wrote in his classic book *Fever Pitch* that Arsenal has often been the great retardant force in his life. I think I proved the same for myself and my relationship with the Bulls in this final collegiate act.

3. April 20, 2009, Bulls vs. Boston Celtics, First round playoffs, Game 2

I was a salaryman in Japan by this point, and had taken my Bulls hooky act overseas. Professional boredom and the identity loss of being an immigrant played a part in this one, though this series was also well on the way to becoming an all-time classic with four overtime games played in a tooth-and-nail seven-game series against the defending champion Boston Celtics.

I'd moved to Tokyo the year before, but was visiting Las Vegas with my company for a big convention that day. Several dozen of my colleagues from Japan had flown in and were in no-nonsense mode, preparing for the nerve-wracking job of having to speak English continuously for the next several days at the company's booth exposition. As the only native English speaker amongst us, they had me on ultra-strict booth duty, and my sole job (remember, I was supposed to be "Director of Sales"!) was to be the designated "English bail-out" guy for anybody struggling with a conversation. I'd sworn to faithfully man the booth, and did just so on the busy first day of the show. I was continuously yanked in as a smiling mouthpiece by my senior managers as their English began to fail them badly during the jet-lagged afternoon hours of the show. But by the second day, I'd had enough.

The Bulls were my escape, once again. Sometime in the afternoon of day two of the show I snuck away from the Las Vegas Convention Center to the next door Renaissance Hotel lobby bar to take in a closely fought game two Bulls loss to the Celtics.

I crystallized my salaryman-version Bulls hooky format on this day: dodging incoming phone calls from frustrated Japanese bosses, and responding to them via text message with vague but legitimate-sounding reasons for my absence.

2. Sunday, March 9, 2014, Bulls vs. Miami Heat, regular season

This Bulls hooky moment flashes forward a few years to when I'd blossomed into a fully-formed, middle-aged Tokyo salaryman. I'd changed companies in Japan a couple of times already, and found that the new place I was at took the idea of the boring, pointless meeting to an entirely different level. I averaged four-plus hours of *insurance-seminar-grade-boring* meetings a day, all in Japanese. It's no wonder I routinely turned to a hustling, overachieving, playoff-bound Bulls team to fill my boredom void.

And so it was that, at 38 years old, and just a month after joining my new company, I found myself sneaking out of an important annual budget meeting and into the office bathroom to watch the Bulls (the game was live on a Tokyo Monday morning)—really the only option to keep my sanity. And there on my smartphone I gorged on the second half of this tasty regular season matchup.

Joakim Noah's career effort – 20 points, 12 rebounds, 7 assists and 4 blocks! – in a thrilling overtime win against LeBron James and the hated Miami Heat repeatedly lifted me off of the Tokyo toilet seat:

1. Friday, May 19, 1989, Bulls vs. Knicks, Game 6, Eastern Conference Semi-Finals

This hooky moment wins on its purity, 1980s nostalgia and general American rough-edged-ness. It reveals where it all started with me, and involves another memorable glimpse at the peak of the Japanese electronics boom. I was at a rural northern Illinois camp ground for a weekend stayover with my eighth grade church classmates. It was for our Confirmation, and we were supposed to be there to officially break from our adolescence and become adult members of the church. The problem for me was the Bulls were also in the middle of their own NBA Confirmation, and were in round two of the playoffs.

It was pre-Internet, pre-cell phone, with an atmosphere full of preachy adults and severely understimulated 13-year-olds. The climactic moment of the Church camp—a campfire lecture by our lead minister—coincided exactly with Game 6 of this heated back-and-forth series with the Knicks, a series that followed Jordan's legendary last-second "The Shot" game that beat Cleveland in the first round.

As I sat there at the churchy campfire that night, my eyes quickly found a similarly Bulls-obsessed friend. He was hiding in a corner of a big group of kids who were seated rectangularly around the campfire. A clever location, I thought. His corner position allowed him to prop his right elbow on his leg and his hand over his right ear, and if you looked closely you could see a suspicious tilt to his head.

I knew the game had just started, and when his eyes met mine from across the campfire, I knew it was just a matter of me figuring out how to maneuver into position to share the other half of that Sony Walkman headphone he was listening to that was tuned to the game's radio broadcast.

He must've panicked at me blowing his cover, because we somehow ended up in the camp latrine to listen to the game. We crouched up on opposite sides of the same toilet seat to hide our feet, a wild-American use case of the now-vintage Walkman, and one that now provides a nice, sad symmetry to my recent Tokyo office bathroom use of the similarly iconic iPhone to watch the Bulls some 30 years later. Legendary Bulls radio announcers Jim Durham and Johnny Kerr were in classic form that night, and it was truly one of the Bulls' franchise-defining games: Jordan won it on two clutch free throws with four seconds left to put the Bulls into the conference finals.

Of course, we heard none of this climatic moment—our jig was up well before Jordan's winning free throws. Sometime at the end of the first half, the door to the latrine was flung open by a search party.

I don't remember the punishment we got, and I hope my naughty, un-Christian actions had nothing to do with the Bulls losing in the conference finals to the Detroit Pistons yet again, which was punishment enough. But at the time it felt like the Bulls and I had crashed and burned together in our Confirmations, and it established my hooky-habit for life.

7

What Happens to the Nail that Sticks Up

THE INTENSE LACK OF SPACE AND FREEDOM that's behind *mottainai* and *basho tori* can beat you down, and besides feeding my lust for the Chicago Bulls, it also fed my American thirst for my own wheels. An intense desire for a Japanese driver's license, and avoiding those packed Tokyo trains as much as possible, drove me into the waiting hands of the Japanese equivalent of the Department of Motor Vehicles.

And that's where I'd learn my next lesson. You see there's an old, well-worn Japanese proverb that kids here absorb in grammar school that comes to hunt down us middle-aged, freedom-seeking Americans in Japan:

> **"The nail that sticks up gets hammered down."**

At the Futamatagawa Driver's License Center near Yokohama, I'd learn that nothing brings out that Japanese hammer quite like the sight of a would-be American driver. A year into immigrating to Japan, thanks to some bad luck, I found myself at Futamatagawa to convert my U.S. driver's license into a Japanese one. My first bit of misfortune was that my apartment at the time jutted into Kanagawa Prefecture by just a few meters—literally. My Kanagawa address meant I couldn't go to the more lenient and foreigner-friendly Tokyo license center.

Then I discovered that every G12 country except the United States had a reciprocal license agreement with Japan—simply fill out some papers and you're done, good to motor the length and breadth of the country. But thanks to a silly U.S.-Japan stalemate—the two countries didn't have a cooperative license agreement with all 50 U.S. states—Americans like me, who already had home-issued licenses, were sent as fodder onto local driving courses to qualify all over again.

The American-trap begins with the fact that Japan's National Police Agency runs the license centers. And the driving course examiners that sit in the car beside you come straight out of a Hollywood teen comedy—totally unbending, humorless police officers. But the final nail in my coffin was Futamatagawa's famously rogue foreign policy, worthy of North Korea. After reading the online rumors about the place, I asked a Tokyo expat relocation firm about it. They replied: "Even when our American clients drive perfectly there, they routinely fail. And they never tell us why."

The Futamatagawa driving course is an oval maze comprised mostly of short straights and ultra-tight turns. The bonsai-like trees and neat grass lining the

THE SALARYMAN

course give it a deceptively calm and simple look. Like many things here in Japan, dangers lurk beneath the calm, Zen-like surface:

I sensed an ambush right before the first test when the examiner handed us the course map. His rapid-fire Japanese explanation of how we were supposed to handle its twists and turns somehow sounded both demanding and vague at the same time:

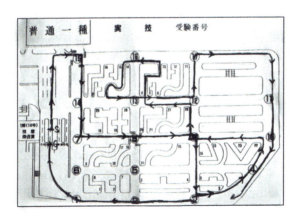

There was another American there named Brian who'd already failed three times, and he had the look of a broken man. When I asked him why he'd failed, he threw his arms up: "I honestly don't know. They won't tell me." Brian then ranted. He said he'd learned you have to wildly exaggerate your every movement during the test so that you appear to be conscientiously following their instructions. So not only should you constantly be swiveling your head to check your side-mirrors, he said you should do it so obviously that your neck cracks. He suggested constant verbal cues—giving a snappy "*Hai!*" ("Yes, OK!") to the examiner in the car—whenever doing anything right on the driving course.

As he kept ranting, he saw it was making me nervous. He thought that a good thing: "They want Americans to look humble". I told him that this all sounded like I was preparing to perform not a driving test, but rather the formal Japanese tea ceremony. But Brian was right. I'd learn that they weren't looking for confident, smooth and safe drivers. They wanted obedient pupils visibly checking off the ritualized rules of their Japanese driving ceremony.

When my name was called for my first test attempt, I jogged up to the examiner with polite, choppy steps. I then bowed and offered him a respectful, "*Yoroshiku onegaishimasu*" ("Please regard me well"). I briefly shuffled my feet, trying to look servile, and then got into the car. A minute later I'd flunked my first attempt at the very start, failing on the first left turn (from the left side of the road, mind you). Their requirement on that turn was that the wheels of the car should never move farther than 70 centimeters from the curb, even while making a turn. Brian and I later laughed at the absurd physics of this, and he nicknamed it the "cartoon car" turn:

The reasoning behind their rule was that hugging the curb in this way blocked bicycle riders—surely suicidal—from sneaking up from your left blind-spot and dangerously rounding the curve with you. But personally I think it was there as just an impossible-to-achieve, sure-to-fail obstacle meant to inject modesty into cocky drivers.

I also learned later, when it was too late, that I'd actually failed on my first attempt before I'd even gotten into the car. You're supposed to get down on your knees and look under the car to make sure no pedestrians were "stuck" under the car before starting the test (apparently this is a popular form of suicide in Japan?). The examiner said nothing of any of these details at the end of my first test. He offered me only a vague, sage-like, "You should get better."

Several failed attempts came my way over the subsequent weeks. To my growing frustration, a different stone-faced examiner would fail me each time on some mysterious errors, with no explanation. I hit rock bottom on test attempt number four. I think I forgot a second mirror check before a lane-change. The examiner clicked his pen and started scribbling, and I snapped at him, "Dammit—come on!" I quickly unraveled, crowning all mistakes on my next turn by maneuvering into the wrong side of the road.

"*Dame desu ne*," ("It's no good, isn't it?") he remarked flatly, instantly failing me. He then steered the car off the course, and I raged at him: "This is BULLSHIT!!"

After my fifth failure (each attempt costing me about 2,500 yen, or $23, and half a day of priceless company holiday), I finally got an explanation after I refused to leave the car. To my surprise, this particular examiner came to life. He shook his head and frowned as he read over my file. He explained that I was a typical American driver. We drive like we're on big, wide roads with little traffic. Japan is different, he said. I thought of *basho tori*, and nodded. True enough. He went on. Americans are too relaxed. They look straight ahead in a lazy-looking, cocky way far too much. Japanese examiners want to see constant effort from their pupils at all times. I should be swiveling my head to the sides and rear even when driving long straightaways. I stifled an objection with a deep breath, and then nodded. *Hai*, I can play that game. Lastly, he said smooth, safe, gradual braking was penalized there for being too casual. This meant that at stop signs I was supposed to pump the brakes furiously so he could "feel" the car "hop" into a sudden, more obvious and *more obedient* stop. At this I lost all patience, and I scoffed loudly. This ended the conversation and he got out of the car.

But just when I thought my rebellion had sentenced me to another five failures in this Japanese gulag, they proceeded to pass me on my next test. And Brian passed on the same day too (his seventh glorious attempt). We both had no idea how we passed, other than that we were possibly viewed by the authorities as being properly humbled by that point.

So I got my Japanese driver's license, and despite all my complaining, to this day I'm still ludicrously proud of it:

Yet I still give any new Kanagawa-based American this piece of advice: avoid the hammer and move to Tokyo. Futamatagawa is no joke.

8

Feed Your Inner Salaryman Beast

THESE HARD OBJECT LESSONS in Japanese culture during my first few years here led me to invent a theory about how the hapless salaryman manages to be so content and polite all the time. It starts with the admirably peaceful Japanese disposition. And a oneness with society that you often find so lacking in the U.S. melting pot. You see, Japan has this *Lord of the Rings* Shire feel to it: isolated, peaceful, and immune to the chaos of the outside world.

I mean, the summer *matsuri* festivals here are the closest thing on Earth to the atmosphere of Hobbits twirling blissfully together to medieval flute music in a forest paradise:

The TV commercials here are soft and peaceful, the totally packed trains are lay-your-head-on-the-passenger-next-to-you's-shoulder-to-sleep peaceful. Even public protests seem pretty peaceful. Japanese even line up and stand in long, uncomfortable lines peacefully and quietly. I can think of no other nationality possessing this enviable trait. Americans can't, won't and don't do any of these things quietly.

I thought back recently to my childhood in order to trace why we Americans lack this peaceful trait. I found, if not the answer, at least an early confirmation of its absence by considering the outdoor summertime games we played growing up. To be fair, we shared many of the same innocent games that Japanese kids play: *Kick the Can*, *Dodgeball*, and Japan even has its own version of *Red Rover*. And I'm sure, for schoolboys, certain games are universal: like who can belch the most letters in the alphabet, variations of the prank *Kancho* (a Japanese version of poking somebody's anus) and who can come up with the best nickname for his junk (for the record, my friend Mike's "Hairy Conan"–he was a Schwarzenegger fan and an early bloomer–barely edged my "Pegasus").

But is there a Japanese middle-class equivalent for the below, borderline-violent suburban Chicago summer games that I played as a kid? It's hard to imagine:

- Hunting squirrels on the grass by jumping down from trees and throwing rocks at them (inspired by the *Rambo: First Blood* wild boar-killing scene)

- Standing on my parent's balcony with my friend Mike and shooting his BB gun at birds (and missing badly)
- A nighttime game created by my neighborhood friend that we called "Mugger", where several of us would line up in straight line and walk around my house repeatedly, staying in a line. The designated mugger would hide in the shadows and proceed to "mug" the person at the very back of our line, one-by-one. The victims weren't allowed to make any sound when they got mugged, and to instill extra terror, you also couldn't look back and see if anyone was still walking in line with you.
- And then there was an original war-play game using fireworks created by my older brother. His name for the game was simple: "Vietnam". Standing on our home's balcony, he'd lob lit Thundercaps at me and my friends below, who had to cross the lawn/battlefield below with only my dad's softball team's bases covering our heads:

So my theory is that my human peaceful gene probably mutated during all this, aided by a childhood full of watching all those bloody Conan and Rambo movies.

. . .

There's nothing in a standard suburban American upbringing that prepares you for Japanese Manner Mode. Case in point, during flu season one of the Tokyo companies I worked for required you to stop and have your body temperature measured by a sensor at the employee entrance before entering (with an HR person standing post at the sensor ready to send you home, the point being that people here simply try to gut everything out and must be told to go home if they have a fever). One time I came to the office with our company's visiting American office manager, and at first she was awed by the sensor technology, which displayed a real-time, color-coded heat map of your face on a big HD screen. But then I stepped to the sensor, and when she saw several other employees waiting in line behind us, gazing at my facial heat map on the screen, she refused to do it. She and the HR guy there got into a loud, confused little tussle over her rights to "personal privacy"—with her trying to break down the Fourth Amendment into a few key words emphasized with dramatic hand gestures—and him finally giving up and waving her through with a frustrated grunt (I was curiously distant from this international tussle for an altogether different reason: I was all for anything that got me out of that office).

Our American visitor's case was instructive. In Tokyo as an adult now, despite all my efforts at immersion, parts of that American Homer Simpson character or wannabe-Rambo boy are still in there somewhere, stewing at being controlled by a company like this. And while sometimes I'm about a packed-train elbow shove in my back away from going Homer on Japanese manners, I sense no fury in the air whatsoever in these cattle-prod situations in Japan. I really believe a big reason is all the retail nurturing going on here.

There's that natural, un-mutated human peaceful trait here, and at the same time an awesome, nurturing Darwin-ish force alive and all around you: the charming stores, restaurants, kiosks, food stands and service manners that pamper you all day in Japan. I see it all as being part of the country's design to absorb the smoldering frustrations of office workers, and keep them at peace.

The beast within all of us salarymen – and our female counterparts – is tamed by retail indulgence, and this is key for living the mannered white-collar lifestyle here. It really does seem like every maddeningly formal blow you take from the Tokyo lifestyle… the beyond-anal rules about throwing out garbage, stuffy offices with thermostats set to 28 degrees, 30 minute office meetings that are made to decide the meeting time of the next meeting, etc. etc…. is countered by some kind of retail delight. There's this great symbiosis between city and man. It ends up making you behave yourself out of pure funk and a drive to score your next little goodie from Tokyo's retail wonderland, such as:

- On your way home from work, a 30 minute foot massage for only 2,000 yen ($18) at a place that's two minutes from your office train station... within 10 minutes of leaving your stuffy work grind you find yourself ensconced in a silk robe with warm towels over your body and face, lying on a bed smelling of lavender and surrounded by faint, soothing music of the forest, followed by an orgasmic Shiatsu session with a climax where they wrap fresh, steaming towels around your calves and unleash an otherworldly chopping and caressing combination on them, and then pull you upright—knocked out and in a comfort coma—and do an unexpected little shoulder-rub encore number on you. You're so relaxed and inert when you checkout that you hand them a 10,000 yen bill ($90) and would've never even noticed if they'd given you a single 1,000 yen note back as change.
- Drinking ice coffee where the ice cubes are made of *coffee,* not water!

- The aromatic Japanese yuzu fruit floating in your hot spring bath (as illustrated below).
- Exploiting the "*Furusato Nozei*" (hometown tax) loophole that diverts part of your Tokyo resident tax into a deductible donation to rural cities of your choice, who then, frothing with gratitude and the Japanese love for gift-giving, ship you piles of locally-made goodies all for a nominal 2,000 yen ($18) fee: rare sweet potato *shochu* and single-malt whiskeys, melt-in-your mouth *unagi* (lake eel), cases of frozen marbled *wagyu* beef and slipper lobsters, and coupons to rural hot spring resorts where a handwritten welcome letter from the local mayor is left on top of the bed to greet you!

THE SALARYMAN

The good vibes from all this delightful consumption—it feels like the Christmas spirit all year round—is one reason 30 million+ Tokyo citizens living in a land area suitable for maybe a million people can take standing on each other's toes every day. It gives everyone the energy to summon all the manners needed to make such an overcrowded city as harmonious as it is.

And at a street level, it's commonly understood how important this consumption force is for the salaryman's sanity. It's a big reason why service is so good in this country, and it drives the common practice for salarymen to create a secret bank account (see Chapter 12) to pay for their retail escapes. This force is also one of the key ways we immigrants tame our frustrations and our wild foreign instincts. We must *try* to indulge in the city as our fellow salaryman do in order to keep our sanity, but doing this can be a messy business for a foreigner.

Take, for instance, the times I'd visit my local *onsen* (hot spring bath) with my two toddler kids. Middle-aged salarymen flock to these places, usually by themselves. For them it's as much about quiet urban refuge and airing their stuff out as it is about ritualistic cleansing and soaking.

Of course I don't get most of the serene benefits enjoyed by Japanese bathers, who sit in total silence and largely ignore each other. I barge in naked and hairy-chested into the packed bath, drawing stares as I'd usually be carrying my daughter in one arm and reining-in my son with the other. My American Family

Man-with-noisy-kids routine seriously tested the limits of their polite and stoic Japanese *wa* (an atmosphere of communal peace and harmony):

And for me there's zero *wa* at first, just a fishbowl feeling that nearly sends me packing. In the outdoor bath, all that would shield me from dozens of curious Japanese eyes was a tiny fig leaf of a washcloth that covered basically nothing (I think this "Free Show", as I call it, that we foreigners must give Japanese bathers should be credited to us and reduce our bath entrance fees).

I've gotten somewhat used to the fishbowl feeling by now, but one particular time when I went to the *onsen* my son snatched my fig leaf from me and ran, utterly exposing me in the merciless daylight. This started a cartoonish sequence where everyone watched a naked, embarrassed white man angrily chase his laughing son around, with his junk flopping up, down and all over.

At this point I almost fell into Homer Mode, and was about to say the hell with Tokyo and its overcrowded *onsen*. But, as always, my fishbowl fever vanished the moment I got into the water. That's the power of a Japanese hot spring. The more stressed out and crazy you feel, the more it rewards you. Like so many charming Japanese retail services that cater perfectly to us insanely tired salarymen, it instantly boomerangs you back to sanity.

It rewards you for giving in to the robotic 8-to-7 Tokyo salaryman grind that turns all of us–foreign and Japanese alike–into the same tame, well-fed beast. A beast that shamelessly needs rest and relaxation at all costs, butt-naked or facial heat map humiliations be damned.

I learned that scoring my little salaryman treats was often just a matter of tapping into my own natural tolerance, and talent, for making an ass out of myself in front of a hundred Japanese, and forgetting about the idea of American personal privacy and dignity. And fortunately nature has blessed me well there.

PART II
DRINKING & OTHER SALARYMAN SKILLS

9

My *Sake* Master

ONCE YOU'RE A CLEAN, well-fed, bathed and well-dressed salaryman, it's time to add a suitable drinking habit to lubricate your yes-man, hard core train commuting lifestyle. Lucky for me, there was a wise, old salaryman in my office to learn from. He was a long-time executive-turned consultant, and had a Tokyo nightlife master reputation. He was from a real dying breed. He was in his late 60s, and had spent nearly 50 years in the electronics industry slaving away with insane working hours, long stints overseas without his family and had survived the long nosedive of the Japanese electronics industry.

Yet there he was still working, and he'd enthrall me with his war stories from his younger days as an engineer in 1960s and 70s Japan. His tales reminded me of the inspired, GDP-driving technologists that I'd read about in the book, *We Were Burning: Japanese Entrepreneurs and the Forging of the Electronic Age.*

He was the epitome of the stoic, patriotic Japanese engineer from that glorious economic age. A talented plow horse for Japan Inc. that was ridden into the ground by his company, he ate, drank and smoked with the best of them while he did it.

Out of respect, a few of us around the office started calling him "the Carnivore" in Japanese, because his tough, consumptive style was in utter contrast to the boring, deflationary young salarymen around us, especially the "*soushoku danshi*" (literally means "herbivore man", a popular term for Japan's modern, timid and withdrawn male office worker).

The Carnivore would scold my more herbivore-like colleagues for their general disinterest in both the virtues and the vices of the traditional salaryman. Basically, he hated that they seemed to have no drive and no toughness, and had the nerve to leave the office before 7pm each night.

He had an emasculating, non-verbal way of dismissing an idea from us younger men: he'd flick his cigarette into the garbage bin in disgust and blow out his smoke as he shook his head. It was especially effective on my herbivore colleagues in the office smoking room, though I also received this treatment at times in our off-site design center, where smoking was allowed at your desk. The popular herbivore smoking fashion in recent years has been Marlboro's IQOS "tobacco heating system", which has a high-tech sheath for the cigarette that heats but doesn't burn the tobacco (creating no secondary smoke and supposedly much healthier; the product was wildly popular in Japan well before it finally got FDA approval in 2019). The Carnivore was totally unimpressed by such advancements and let the herbivores know it:

I was tied to the Carnivore on a project for eight months at a tiny off-site design office far from our headquarters, and it was there that he personally put me on his junior Carnivore training program. I remember one October night, as a typhoon was bearing down on Tokyo, I helplessly stayed with him doing quality checks on a piece of electronics he was designing. I remember pleading to him, "All of Tokyo is fleeing to their homes for cover and the trains are shutting down!" He simply lifted his fierce, fuzzy head up from the circuit board he was soldering and frowned at me, disgusted at the idea of leaving work unfinished for a mere category 3 typhoon.

There were few words: I knew I wouldn't be leaving. We worked all night through the typhoon, and later slept on office chairs that we put together in a row. In the morning we went to the local bathhouse to clean up before coming right back to the office, a workaholic style that the Carnivore seemed to relish, as he said it reminded him of his heyday.

Another time, he bullied me into going to an unheated far Tokyo suburban warehouse on a mid-winter Saturday morning to replace the faulty microchips inside several hundred units of a stereo system our company had hastily shipped out. Despite my initial protests, I was surprisingly at ease once I settled into our makeshift two-man production line. The way he could instantly pop open a stereo chassis cleanly and unhinge a microchip on its circuit board without scratching anything, while at the same time watching what I was doing and shouting directions, and between times humming snatches from the opera *Carmen,* was beyond all praise.

At that moment, I understood his value as a troubleshooting audio engineer and why my company had hired him. I also realized, after asking him if he'd rather be doing something else on a weekend, that for him this was a fleeting chance to proudly keep using skills honed long ago during a time when Japan was the global force in consumer electronics. He couldn't face the void of retirement after 50 years in the trenches, which was a far more depressing thought for him than applying his great skills on an unworthy product in a dark, depressing warehouse on a Saturday.

Nine other things you didn't know about the Carnivore:

- He refused to use air conditioning in his Tokyo home for more than two years after the big 2011 East Japan earthquake. He did it out of a self-imposed discipline to help with Japan's post-quake power shortage, despite the need for such rationing being lifted several months after the quake.
- He designed a top-selling home karaoke system for his audio manufacturer employer in the 1970s. To do this, he worked more than 90 hours a week over a two-year period while smoking a pack of unfiltered cigarettes a day.
- Through his connections in the music industry, he claimed he attended a big Tokyo going-away party for a pre-famous Yoko Ono in the mid-1960s.
- He travelled the world in the 1970s and 80s recording jazz and classical music for his company's music label, and a 1987 article in the New York Times Art section called him a "physicist with a passion for music".
- As an executive several years later, he got kicked out of this same company after he, in a fit of patriotism, tried to undermine his board's decision to be acquired by American private equity.
- Since this falling out with his old company more than twenty years ago, he'd tried without

success to start his own businesses, and then mostly bounced around in random consulting assignments, unable to overcome the stench that even a single failure holds in ultra-conservative corporate Japan. He said to me once with a deep sigh: "I used to know this American entrepreneur; I'd bump into him every few years at events in the States. All his ventures would fail, but every time I saw him he was wearing a nicer suit."

- One time, while we were in the middle of giving a presentation together to a room full of American customers, he suddenly flipped out and, in front of the audience, blasted me for being too casual and disrespectful in my manner. His gripe: I'd forgotten that I represented a Japanese employer, and while standing up had put my thumbs in my front pant pockets in the casual American-guy style, rather than standing upright with my hands clasped obediently behind my back as a Japanese would do while listening to customers.
- He was a charming, globally-minded, fluent English-speaking gentleman when sober, but when drunk he turned into a fierce right-wing economic patriot, with me once hearing him yell: "They should kick all of these foreign software companies out of Japan!"
- He grew up in a decimated post-World War II Tokyo in the late 1940s/early 50s, sleeping in

un-air conditioned grade school dorms. Another reason we gave him the Carnivore nickname was because of a vivid childhood memory he shared with us from his days in the old Tokyo slums: he was standing in line at this cheap street curry stand that he loved, when a gust of wind suddenly revealed why their sauce had so much juicy meat in it:

. . .

The Carnivore balanced my hard-core daytime work lessons with a nighttime role as my kindly old *sake* master. At our first dinner together, he quickly established our master/protégé relationship with, "I'd already been drinking *sake* for 30 years when you were still learning how to put your pants on!"

We spent many nights together at local taverns, where he'd patiently let me air my complaints about Japanese business culture while we methodically soaked in his favorite *sake*.

He'd earned a *sake* master reputation through years of wining and dining customers during Japan's 1980s economic heyday. He had his tough carnivore style internally at the company, but to foreign customers he was your classic white-collar gentleman relic from that era: a well-mannered, English-speaking patriot with high-end tastes who would grind out deals late into the night for the company. In his 1980s prime, behind that cultured façade was a brutal, hard-to-read international negotiator with a distinguished executive *gaijin* (foreigner) kill-list, aided by his famous cast-iron liver:

For years he enjoyed his own *"bottle-keep"*–his own private bottle of special high-end *sake* kept only for him–at many of the best restaurants within walking distance of his office. In his prime he used this, and his ability to drink quarts of alcohol and still keep a conversation, to close big deal after big deal for his company.

These are still coveted Japanese business skills, but their glory is all in the past. He stayed on with his old company after the economic bubble burst in the 1990s, a fierce loyalty keeping him there despite his salary being cut by nearly half. His financial free-fall in the past two decades forced him–and a whole generation of salarymen like him–towards more low-end tastes. In his mid-50s by then, his legendary drive had left him, and he dealt with his boredom by finding "value *sake*". I felt lucky to score some of these wise value *sake* nuggets from him.

At the time I knew him, he swore by a fine *futsuu-shu* (economical) Niigata *sake* named Hakkaisan Futsushu (he described it as "Dry, light and fruity", and I believe my post-sip reply the first time was, "Damn!"). I viewed this value *sake* as like a Japanese equivalent to Spanish wine. He viewed it, in his helpless professional state at the time, as a sort of amniotic fluid. Still, he'd sometimes longingly nod at the high-end *sake* list on the menu and, at remembering that he didn't have a company entertainment expense account or bottle-keep anymore, he usually frowned and sadly light a cigarette. Then he's usually floor me with his gluttonous stories from the bubble days.

One time I recall him masterfully diverting a conversation I started with a typical foreigner complaint, "I think having to be so polite all the time is actually making me sick...", into a lesson on high-end *sake* brewing. Unlike *futsuu-shu sake*, he interrupted me, high-end sake uses special techniques to mill away the outer portions of rice grains, which are full of fats and proteins that hinder flavor. This allows a higher-concentration of the tasty starches at the center of the grain to get through.

My *sake* master said that he knew the 1980s bubble was officially over when he was forced to come down to "fatty, crap *futsuu-shu*", as he called it. He swatted away the recent low-cal Japanese *shochu* (distilled alcohol from rice or sweet potato) Hi-Ball cocktail craze–"Ha! Diet *sake*. Stuff for office ladies and herbivore men", he croaked. This bad *sake*, plus all the greasy tavern food and the stress, led to gout attacks that started just before I met him in the late 2000s.

There was many a sad, comical morning my first year in the company when he'd limp in on a gouty foot after a long night out. I remember one time half the office guiltily stifling laughs as he muttered to our receptionist, "Oh... my... God, my gout!"

The next year, after a long period of careful dieting, we were invited to celebrate his "Comeback from Gout", as he grandly called it in an email invitation, an event that also doubled as my goodbye party as I had recently announced I was leaving the company. He gloriously returned that night to an old premium *sake* favorite, the Dassai brand, which has a fascinating high-end rice-grain production method that uses the very traditional method of purely brewing from rice and not adding any distilled alcohol.

In a nod to me, the only Westerner present, he opted for Dassai's progressive sparkling *sake,* and with that masterful stroke he capped my Carnivore training with an inspired twist.

10

Empty Stomach Boozing 101

THE INTIMATE ONE-ON-ONE *SAKE* master sessions were a great stepping-stone to handling the standard company drinking marathons that come with Japanese salarymanhood. The drive for these nocturnal blitzes starts with the utter formality of working at a traditional Japanese company. I once worked at a Japanese factory for a year, and the place had a fanatical focus on quality control and office rules, leading to a palpable undercurrent of pent-up employee frustration. Every activity of the day there dripped with officious formality:

- An office PA recording would guide us through mandatory light calisthenics every morning at 8:25AM sharp.
- This would be followed by our morning line-up, where our team each day would stand in a circle and go around one-by-one reading a rule from the company's rulebook (the HR department took great joy in producing an English translation of it for me). Some memorable rules I noted were:

Rule #19: ***Employees may not engage in any conduct that violates rules designated by the written pledges or the instructions of their superiors***. Despite the laughable rule and the yes-man image of the salaryman, the reality is that idiot bosses are ignored here too, but just in a more subtle and polite way.

Rule #39: ***Employees may not refuse a job transfer to another city or country***. This one is followed almost without exception, and explains the whole society of salarymen involuntarily living apart from their families for years at a time.

Rule #47: ***Employees may not make improper expense requests for personal expenditures or by submitting false reports.*** The irony of this one is that HR departments at many Japanese companies, and all the ones I worked for, do everything they can to help their male employees create questionable business trips just to create expense reimbursements that hides their post-work, nighttime spending from their wives (see Chapter 12).

- We started *every* weekly division meeting by reciting our company's mission statement with a forced-enthusiasm that was suitable for a North Korean TV news telecast.
- And of course the standard guilt you felt at asking for a day or two off, which led to you

bowing gravely to your boss when asking for his approval:

I once counted the number of times I gave some kind of servile bow or apologized for some small error in the factory in a day, and it was more than 20.

This kind of Manner Mode formality in the office is meant to make everyone more comfortable, and it does, if you're Japanese. But to overwrite such etiquette onto your natural American casualness is an intimidating exercise. For example, take something as simple as saying goodbye to an office visitor. In the U.S., the "business goodbye" flows with the context of the meeting, and runs the gamut from…

"... Thanks for coming, here's your parking validation, you remember how to get out?"

to

"Cool man, see you next month!"

to

"I'm calling security. Release the hounds!"

In Japan, the choreography of the goodbye is *always* done in the same polite and perfect manner, no matter the situation. You follow your visitor all the way out to the elevator when they leave, exchange bows just before the elevator door closes, and *hold your bow until the elevator closes all the way*. This sounds easy enough, but its execution actually takes perfect timing–and a lot of teeth-clenching if the meeting basically wasted your time–that can only be honed from a disciplined Manner Mode upbringing (I don't even attempt it anymore). You need timing for when you bow vs. when the guest bows, for how deep you bow, and, most critically, for not getting your head thumped by the closing elevator door as happened to me once:

THE SALARYMAN

After dealing with these formalities all day, we were usually ready to hit the Tokyo *izakaya* (bistro, tavern) around 8pm. We'd be coasting on the fumes of the bento box lunches provided by the factory, because when working at a Japanese factory you aren't allowed to leave the building for a snack, and of course can't eat at your desk. The daily fasting took a bigger toll on me than on my co-workers, who were used to it and would cheat hunger every afternoon by smoking their heads off in the company smoking room:

As an American you're basically working with a metabolic handicap: lacking a smoking habit and having grown up in a Supersize-me food culture, your system simply isn't wired for such discipline. When we all sat down at the *izakaya* at night, I'd feel like a vegetable and my stomach would be about to eat itself. Holy drinking hell would immediately be unleashed, and there was never any eating of greasy appetizers to line your stomach and protect you. Instead, lots of little, shared dishes would make an appearance on the table, and always get quickly washed away by an all-you-can-drink *tsunami* of beer, *sake* and *shochu*. Nobody had eaten anything for more than seven hours, yet somehow they were always content to pick at skinny *yakitori* chicken skewers, *edamame*, and little *soba* noodle dishes.

In these tavern situations, my Western stomach always yearned for some greasy Manfood like chicken wings or fries, or at least a basket of table bread. I distinctly remember one time at one of these all-you-can-drink "dinners" that the only entrée our boss ordered for six of us were a few cute, tea saucer-sized pizzas. The pizzas landed on the table, and were within my arm's reach, but I correctly restrained myself and let my superiors have first crack at them. After all, these were men who could've the next day, if they felt like it, decided by themselves that they were transferring me to the company's suddenly-opened branch office in *Pakistan*. And because of rules like Rule #39 from our company's rulebook, which makes refusing a job transfer grounds for discipline, there'd have been nothing I could've done about it.

I considered this as I watched them nibble on business card-sized pizza slices with their chopsticks for a couple minutes while I thought, "God I want to FUCKING DESTROY that pizza". I imagined folding two pieces together while nobody was looking and throwing it down in one mouthful, but gave up on the idea out of pure salaryman funk.

The *izakaya* two-hour all-you-can-drink course is a true salaryman special. After getting drunk, smoking is the second priority, with actual food being tertiary. For the first half of these dinners, I'd usually fight off my hunger with *edamame* and orders of *sake*. On the positive side, the tension of the office grind dissipated once the alcohol settled in, and my colleagues' Jekyll and Hyde transformation from formal rule-followers to jolly dinner companions was always instant:

Once the beer started flowing with the same people I was bowing all day to, a sudden change would always come over them. The ties loosened. The set of their shoulders relaxed. People talked at the top of their voices and tried to capture the conversation. Opinions, even gripes about the company, were fired off freely in the boozing boss' direction, who always listened with good humor. This huge, instant temperature swing somehow always reminded me of that old Church hymn that mentions both Greenland's icy mountains and India's coral strand.

The formality that ruled over us all day would then seem a world away once our party reached the karaoke room:

In the end, it turns out all this food deprived-boozing is to your benefit, and I probably should be ashamed of complaining as much as I have. I mean, as a middle-aged Western immigrant, you have to take your medicine if you want to tap into Japan's world-leading average life expectancy. And apparently getting regularly drunk on an empty stomach is part of the artery-clearing prescription for longevity. It may also be part of Japan's grand economic plan anyway to force-diet its flabby Western residents into buying all that slim-cut Cool Biz Japanese clothing, which isn't such a bad thing.

All in all, the lesson the Japanese company all-you-can-drink dinners finally teach you is that all this heavy daytime formality and food discipline is a fine excuse to drink a fish tank of liquor guilt-free at night. It's one of the sacred perks of Tokyo salaryman life.

11

The Foreign Guest Honey Trap

THE DINNER BOOZE FESTS can also be flipped into a sneaky home-field business advantage when foreign guests are visiting. Now don't get me wrong, Japan's reputation of world-class hospitality is very well-earned. It's just that, well, sometimes a dinner is not just a dinner. It's a well-coordinated feast driven by motivations that are more serious than many visiting foreign businesspeople realize. Basically, what's happening here is an elaborate, unspoken transaction: the foreigner's entertainment tonight in exchange for a Japanese business victory the next day.

And I've often been called on by my bosses to lure my compatriots into this honey trap by being a double-agent traitor, and not warning them. At the heart of this is the wicked Japanese ability to own all of the delicious details of a big business dinner feast, even while they join in on the gorging at the same time. This is especially true when Japanese companies are involved. They take the hospitable business dinner to an absolute art form, and it ought to be listed as intellectual property on their balance sheets.

Many visiting foreigners who know Japan well greedily write-off this trade as part of doing business here. As a prized job perk. But the nocturnal honey trap seduces Japan newbies unknowingly. Even in these cases, I'd argue, the trade-off of losing the business negotiation the next day is usually worth it. Japanese hospitality is that amazing.

In the case of the newbie American business guest who falls for the honey trap, more times than not it's a middle-aged man. And it typically proceeds as follows.

He'll put on his tough businessman face on when he greets his Japanese hosts in his hotel lobby before dinner. But then he'll proceed to get completely disarmed by everybody's attention to his personal comfort. The guest first does a double take at the young, cute ladies who handle his bags at the hotel. He contrasts that image with the brusque, tip-seeking male valets in U.S. hotels, and watches in awe as they bow at him to apologize for touching his belongings. He gushes as he thanks one of them, and she finishes him off with a smile and a flattering comment in broken English. This un-glues the American, and he gets so disoriented by the existence of such cute, pert manners from hotel baggage handlers that he mistakes the whole gesture. "Dude, I think she wants me," he says matter-of-factly to me, his fellow American.

I tend to play Mr. Japan Expert at these moments, and wave him off: "Man, that's just normal Japanese service. It's just so much better than the U.S. that it kinda seems like flirting." Then my company's hosts set their hooks into him with the paid-for hotel spa treatment and a foot massage. And then the hosts design the evening's dinner feast so that he doesn't even have to bother with the servers. Without lifting a finger, he finds himself gorging on the amazing Okinawan beer and a whole starter kit of Japanese dishes.

Then the host for the evening, my middle-aged Japanese vice president boss, takes over. With his right hand clutching a *sake* bottle, the host keeps the foreigner's other cup topped at all times while also keeping the table's charming conversation trained on *him,* the guest.

The foreigner is then hooked, and proceeds to follow his host's impressive lead with the food and booze. The host's left hand is a whirl of consumption, alternating between chewing on *yakitori*, wiping his greasy fingers on an *oshibori* cloth and working a cigarette, yet at the same time he still has the awareness to refill the guest's sake cup effortlessly from across the table:

When the *sake* bottle hits empty, the host immediately jolts the waitress into action from *across the*

room with three straight calls of "sumima-SEHNNN!" (excuse me!), with a growing stress each time on the "SEH" sound that, in Japanese tavern dialect, implies impatience. He growls playfully at the waitress when she arrives with a new bottle 20 seconds later, "*Jikai, motto haiyaku dayo!*" (next time faster!), and at this she politely bows.

It's all a display of awesome Japanese hosting instincts, organized relaxation, and of how in everyday Tokyo life an elder salaryman is allowed to take utter proprietorship over a restaurant to his own liking. The foreign guest thinks of how an American waitress would've probably reacted by pouring a hot bowl of soup in this guy's lap.

And then, minutes later, as the foreigner leans back in his seat in awe of it all, the host takes it up yet another notch. He tells the waitress to bring him his personal bottle of single-malt Yamazaki whisky on "*botteru kippu*" (bottle keep) at this *izakaya*. He then casts off the *sake* bottle to a subordinate–as in "here, you guys drink that stuff"–while he and the foreigner begin to soak in the special Yamazaki.

Everyone seems perfectly happy, and it hits the foreigner that this "foreign guest *izakaya* experience" not only belongs in the Tokyo tourist guidebooks, but deserves its very own chapter. The whole understated servitude of it all is an ego-boost; how everything you say or do is funny and interesting, way funnier and more interesting than you ever seem in the U.S., even as you grow grotesquely overfed and drunk.

It all starts to go to the foreigner's head, and at one point the waitress giggles at his slurred attempt at Japanese, and says something in return in Japanese with a smile. He asks his host what she said, and when he jokes, "Take off your pants!", the foreigner takes it half-seriously. The whole feast is tilted this way; it's a brilliantly subtle ploy to overstimulate the guest with flattery, food and booze.

As the night winds down, a small doubt about the big price negotiation with this Japanese host the next morning creeps in. But the foreigner dismisses it with, "Nah, it's in the bag, look at the way he's treating me!" The night then extends well beyond midnight, but I'd been party to too many of these honey traps to enjoy them anymore, as I start to visualize the self-destructive results for this American guest the next day. I bail after the check comes and the party moves on to the next bar.

Sleeping is delicious that night for the American guest, but he wakes up with hot coals in his head and a disturbing realization. The long flight the day before, the arranged hot Japanese spa and massage, and then the boozy dinner; it all has left him totally dehydrated and bloated. He glances at his hotel toilet and with a moan exclaims to himself, "Jesus, I haven't taken a dump in like three days!"

Arriving at the host's office that morning, the tables quietly continue to turn. The hangover, the constipation, the miraculously chipper-looking host and the very hot, bright offices are all foreboding signs. The foreigner starts to wonder if something else besides hospitality was going down last night too. He stifles some stomach pain and fumbles with his meeting agenda, unable to concentrate.

His normal pre-meeting preparations are constantly interrupted by the Japanese company's cute, immaculately mannered lady receptionists, who hound him in halting English for business cards, hotel receipts, and various other minor stuff. He awkwardly deals with all this; his physical condition and this interference completely distract him from his normal meeting preparations. Much to his annoyance, he's more focused on showing good manners than he is on the business at hand. Yet all they're doing is continuing to show great attention to HIM, so he can't complain. But he realizes that it also distracts him from the negotiation, and with some realization setting in, he wonders to himself half-jokingly, "I bet they even planned my constipation!", closer than he realizes to the truth.

It won't occur to him until later on his flight home, while writing up the trip summary for his boss, that he got honey-trapped. But that would be too late. The foreigner is hurting bad and way off his game, and also now finds himself emotionally in debt to his— somehow totally chipper!—host for the previous night. (Note: Another home field advantage that tilts the playing field toward the Japanese: access to their pharmaceutical industry's arsenal of cutting-edge hangover cures. Tonics with turmeric root that jackhammer the toxins out of your liver, late-night ramen snacks with broth that's full of clam juice laced with amino acids that crush alcohol, health drinks spiked with the antioxidant taurine–it's all part of the secret Japanese honey trap game plan. The limp Westerner visitor is helpless versus these kinds of Asian white-collar steroids).

My Japanese bosses then proceed to feast on him at the negotiating table. They turn up the temperature in the room on purpose, stonewall his questions with vague English answers surrounded by long passages in Japanese, and exploit his hangover by extending the meeting beyond four hours:

The bloated, sweating, foreign guest finally gives in with, "Jesus H Christ. A 20% price cut. OK! Fine! Just let me out of here!"

Then the Japanese smiles from the previous night return, as the foreigner has returned their dinner favor in the form of their honey trap victory. And the transaction—with my Japanese company's management blowing the deal's ink dry before the foreign guest gets home and gathers his wits—is complete.

12

The Secret Cash Stash

ALL THIS NOCTURNAL CONSUMPTION begs the question: how exactly does today's famously deflation-bit salaryman pay for all this? Certainly, there's no time and freedom to have a second income. The Tokyo salaryman utterly surrenders such freedom in the name of lifetime employment to the company. The answer, I discovered, was that there's a hidden, intricate entrepreneurialism buried in salaryman society that generates the needed funds. All those company rules, the kowtowing to idiot bosses, the social pressure to attend company drinking parties…all this leads to the common salaryman practice of building a secret money stash. This practice is known as *hesokuri* (literally *"money hidden in the navel"*), and it's one of Japan's secret salaryman survival tools.

It works as a kind of Freedom Fund for salarymen. The inspiration? Restoring personal sanity with off-family-balance-sheet detours into Tokyo's retail wonderland: "Many Japanese salarymen have a secret bank account," said an executive at my company when I emailed him about making my own *hesokuri*. "There are so many ways to use it, and it actually is basic policy for Japanese companies to support it."

Hesokuri is a term that's been around since the Edo period of Japanese history. It traditionally was equated with money that housewives secretly stashed away for shopping and dining. But that definition was more applicable to the economic bubble period of the late 1970s and 1980s, when huge corporate expense accounts funded the salaryman's hedonistic entertainment and housewives raided their husbands' fat company bonuses for spending money.

From what I've seen, two decades of economic stagnation have drastically altered the use of *hesokuri*. The stakes these days are much lower—big expense accounts are gone and fat bonuses are rare, so the modern housewife has slim pickings. So now it's the pinched salaryman who quietly and methodically creates a *hesokuri* with skimmed slivers of cash. In the places I've worked, *hesokuri* has been a natural expression of accumulated, unexpressed employee frustration. When work is finally over, the tension is explosively released—never belligerently, but rather with an earnest feeling shared with co-workers, like hats being thrown in the air together. I wish I could find a bar in the US half as cheery as the typical *izakaya*.

Still, you won't find *hesokuri* listed in any Japanese company's handbook. In the beginning, I got wind of it from a veteran manager who sat next to me. His enthusiasm was instructive.

He leaned over in his chair and whispered conspiratorially in English: "If *hesokuri* yes …", he made a motion of upending a bottle and sucked noisily. "If *hesokuri* no …", he made a choking sound and pretended to slash his lower stomach with a sword in the manner of *seppuku*, the samurai ritual suicide by disembowelment. He then pointed over to the desk of my boss, indicating he'd hook me up if I wanted: "Go get *hesokuri*. You very like."

The way it works, I learned, is they first create a secret account at one of those paper-statement-less Japanese Internet banks. This keeps things separate from the family bank account that receives the monthly company paycheck and business expense reimbursements, my boss explained. This secret account is the foundation of *hesokuri*, as most married men essentially turn over their family bank account to their wives, who control household spending and from it dole out a monthly *kozukai* (their "official" personal-spending allowance) to their husbands. (Important note: this is a common scenario for households where only the husband works. Dual-income families were not the norm in the Japanese companies I worked).

A disciplined salaryman can live within the typical wife's *kozukai* budget—about 35,000 yen ($325) per month and shrinking every year, according to news reports—but it's a very tricky business. Most of my colleagues weren't equal to the effort after all the clenched rule following they do all day at work. After all that Manner Mode effort, resisting the gleaming vending machines, station kiosks, bars and cafés that charmingly line every step of the exhausting Tokyo commute is almost impossible. As is evading all the *kozukai*-busting enticements, and they're everywhere in dense, uber-expensive Tokyo—the *nomikai* (office drinking parties), fancy lunch invitations from fat-cat managers and pit stops at pricey cafés after customer sales calls. You could multiply these situations by a thousand; it's all part of the challenge of staying within a wife's *kozukai* budget in Tokyo.

Group pressure, waves of temptation and the general funk that builds from trying to say no are usually enough for even the most earnest salaryman to cave in and create a *hesokuri*. At the very least, it's hard to deny its use as a backup fund, as I have at times. Many, including me, simply have used it to prevent the embarrassment of saying no to a senior colleague's drinking invitation– saying you don't have enough *kozukai* is a little emasculating and will raise an eyebrow or two. It is for this face-saving reason—and avoiding unpleasant financial conversations with the wife about the *kozukai*—that a fair number of my colleagues have resorted to *hesokuri*.

But it's also true that a surprising number of them take it much further and swindle their wives wholeheartedly. One of the middle-aged sales managers at my previous firm, for instance, used to have the company dump all of his business-trip expense reimbursements into his secret bank account, blatantly testing the limits of his wife's obliviousness. A friend of mine, I clearly remember his sad story the day after his *hesokuri* bubble-era ended. He told me: "My wife finally caught me last night. She screamed, 'You had many business trip expense in Osaka and America last month, but your salary payment was the same! Please explain! You must explain.'"

The company then conspired to let my friend funnel off smaller, less noticeable parts of his expense reimbursement. He chose the daily meal allowance of 3,500 yen given on business trips. Younger colleagues with more attentive wives also preferred skimming from the meal allowance because it was off the top, so to speak, and therefore virtually undetectable. If you take frequent business trips and opt for cheap convenience-store bento meals on the road, they explained, the profit can work as an airtight, untraceable, all-cash *hesokuri* (note: I got frequent invitations to drink and carouse all night, which would've possibly ruined me financially and definitely ruined me physically, so I invented the perfect excuse, one that satisfied the salaryman expectation of American vitality in these areas: "Guys, if I turn my beast mode on, I'm afraid I won't be able to turn it off.")

The clever salaryman has a more sophisticated, credit card-based way of skimming his *hesokuri*. My colleagues sheepishly described it as a *jidensya sogyo* (a bicycle operation), which is an expression that refers to the financial juggling act of running a small business on a shoestring budget. The image of it resembles the frantic pedaling of a stationary bike.

With this method, they'd start their bicycle operation by using the company credit card to pay for both regular business expenses and their wife-sensitive night-prowling expenses (they naturally had the credit card statements sent to the office and not their home). The company automatically paid the credit card balance immediately at the end of the month on behalf of the employee, including the personal expenses. The employee then quickly filed their business expense report and would get reimbursed immediately for that on their next paycheck, while the personal expenses would be deducted from the *following month's* paycheck. That 4- or 5-week grace period – created by the company reimbursing business expenses faster than it deducts for personal expenses–is the standard conspiratorial benefit you get at Japanese companies, and is the key to the whole *hesokuri* dodge. It gives salarymen a "pedaling period" to generate enough *new* business expenses to cover up the *previous month's* personal expenses. If he doesn't pedal hard enough, then the wife would surely notice the dent in the next month's paycheck, and the game would be up:

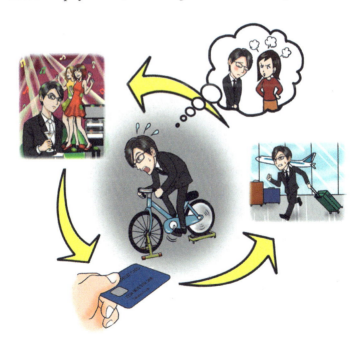

The final conspiratorial piece is the typical Japanese company's lenient attitude toward business trips and customer entertainment expenses, the twin engine that drives *hesokuri*. Many a questionable business trip to some distant customer or factory is done for *hesokuri* purposes, and there's a national salaryman-to-salaryman understanding between Japanese suppliers and their customers that allows for the practice of *aisatsu* meetings (meetings without a specific agenda and merely done for appearances, and often expense-generation). These trips would generate 3,500 yen/day ($30) in per diem at my company, always a popular bicycle operation equalizer, as well as a 9,000 yen/night ($85) accommodation fee the company paid for hotels, which could be turned into a small profit if you opt for a no-frills, 3,500 yen/night capsule hotel where you sleep in something the size of a large casket.

The reality is that this half-drunk, half-panicked *hesokuri* mode requires a great deal of daily concentration for many salarymen. It has a Sword of Damocles effect that I noticed generated great energy, energy that could've been useful for the company if only they provided any productive ways to use it. Professional boredom is at the bottom of *hesokuri*, and it's hard to blame the salaryman for dealing with a motivational vacuum that they didn't create. Still, on the positive side, whenever global economists rail about Japan's lost decades of stagnation, I think it misses an important silver lining. That the culture here has always funneled lost productivity into a humming retail industry using all this salaryman *hesokuri* innovation.

But, as with any economic loophole, things can easily get out of hand. There was an engineer at my company who had a 40,000 yen ($375) a month *kozukai* from his wife that was wholly inadequate for his appetites. The budget didn't come close to satisfying his taste for "soaplands" (naughty massage parlors), so he boldly went for the *hesokuri* home run twice a year using a very clever trick. Every July and December, he'd have the company send his bonus – each equal to some two months of salary – to his secret bank account and then proceed to skim a sizable portion for himself. On the same day, he then would send the rest of the bonus to his family account by bank transfer. The key to the deception? He manually changed the 'sender' name in the wire transfer from his secret bank's name to our company's name.

Not quite believing what I was seeing, I once asked a Japanese friend at a major trading company about *hesokuri*. He explained it was basically the same there at his company, with an added conspiratorial twist— his company gave employees an end-of-year "special bonus" check skimmed from their official company bonus. Going for anywhere between 100,000 yen to 300,000 yen ($900-$3,000) each year, the special bonus checks were typically cashed at a bank for secret nocturnal rampages.

How can a check that big possibly go unnoticed by a wife? Here's how: Japanese companies deduct income tax on all salary payments and file their employees' income-tax returns for them (basically, only the rich or self-employed must file their own individual returns in Japan). So this automatic tax return filing by the employer means a wife doesn't ever see the discrepancy between a husband's bank-deposited salary and his *recorded income* at the local tax office.

And poof! That's the way a salaryman's annual bonus magically disappears from the family ledger, and instead lands in the bars, restaurants and coffee shops of Japan.

13

American Manner Buffer

ALL THE STRESS OF THIS SECRECY, rule-following and office formality are reasons most Japanese salarymen love overseas business trips. It's a huge pressure valve for them. But there's always a culture and language gap that comes with this too. And as an American in a Japanese company in Japan, one of your unspoken duties is to be a buffer between American manners and your bosses during US business trips. Your job is to shield them from the foreign wilderness, and keep them with one foot in their comfort zone.

The reward for this is that you occasionally get to see their comfort zone yanked out from under them and watch them react spontaneously, which *never* happens in Japan. And sometimes when this happens you see buried talents emerge.

On one trip, I remember the challenge of my buffer duties hitting me as I watched my boss at Tokyo Haneda airport let a security lady gently take off his coat and fold it for him as he walked through the scanner. She bowed deeply and apologized to him for the inconvenience of… airport security.

It was the presuming way he nodded his head at her that struck me, as a satisfied lord might nod to a servant. It seemed he almost expected her to next hand him one of those little Japanese wet towels to wipe his hands:

The pampering effect of Japanese service truly creates a cocoon, I thought, and it extended into the Japan Airlines lounge, where my boss scoffed at the selection of wines and then stirred the staff there into apologetic action when a buffet item was temporarily unavailable. On the flight, I watched him fuss with a JAL flight attendant over the slippers they gave him in his Premium Economy seat. Apparently they weren't on par with business class, and the attendant bowed deeply and quickly retrieved him a better pair from the front of the plane.

It all showed again how Japanese businessmen are blessed with this awesome sense of proprietorship over their domestic retail industry. I imagined what a United Airlines flight attendant would've done. Poured a cup of coffee down his back, probably.

The rattling of his Japanese manner cocoon began with the standard-issue, Teamster-like US immigration officers that greet you when you get off the plane. "NEXT!!!", barked an annoyed-looking, ruddy-faced heavyset lady when we got to LAX immigration. My startled boss fumbled with his papers, and she sighed at him impatiently.

Welcome to the USA, I thought.

My boss had often complained that greasy, American fast food seemed to be the only option at mealtime on previous trips, so I had planned ahead and found a salad/soup buffet for lunch that first day. At lunch, I saw him struggling over in the restaurant's soup area, squinting at a soup name and then asking the lady behind the counter: "What this please?" She replied enthusiastically in a thick Polish accent: "Es mine-stroo-ne. Ess goo-du. You schude tuu-rye!" He twisted his head in confusion and looked over at me, his manner buffer. So, I ran over and translated: "Minestrone. She said it's good. You should try".

The US melting pot was a shock to his system; daily Japanese life is completely unfettered with foreign accents. He found it charming and left her an unexpected tip afterwards, despite his general loathing of the US tipping system. This stemmed from his one time in Las Vegas, when he locked himself out of his hotel room and asked the cleaning lady outside his room to let him back in. She paused, looked him up and down, and made a "cough up some money" rubbing motion with her forefinger and thumb. He was late for a meeting, didn't have me his manner buffer with him, and felt no choice but to give her $5 to open up the room. After this, he swore off all tipping in all non-restaurant situations—a nerve that I admired—and even at meals he'd leave only 10% – a nerve I didn't admire, because I usually absorbed baleful looks from American waiters on his behalf.

On this trip, we met up with our local Japanese staff and visited our L.A. customer, a laid-back, cool and casually mannered California electronics company director. My boss entered their conference room, and was locked-in on the business card exchange.

It was their first time to meet, and these situations are highly ritualized in Japan: a little small talk, approach each other with your card in both hands in front of you, step right, step left, stiff handshake, and then a servile two-handed delivery of your card. Of course, more worldly Japanese businessmen ease up a lot on their formality when outside of Japan. But not this boss. He sat there stuck at the "step left" stage and was partially bent over, as if he was frozen in the act of extending his hand. The American was blabbering on and in mid-story about something, oblivious that this little Japanese ceremony was going on. My boss stood there looking wide-eyed at him, not listening. I sighed to myself: neither side was communicating.

THE SALARYMAN

This is the essence of life as an American working at a Japanese company.

After I stepped in to untie this little entanglement, the meeting went longer than expected. When it was over and we got into our rental car, the Japan office was just beginning their workday over in Tokyo, and already pestering my boss via texts for official updates on our meeting. His plan had been to unwind inside the cocoon of an authentic local Japanese restaurant in L.A., but this was now impossible: now he had to go back to the hotel to prepare for a conference call with our president that night. The dual pressure of all this casual American-ness and Japanese formality pressed on him, and he snapped: "Time for *ham-bah-gah*!"

He swerved the car into the first drive-thru he saw, deciding dinner would be hamburgers eaten in the car during rush hour on the way back to our hotel. He asked openly whether to get cheese on everything: "Hmmm. Cheddar burger. Cheddar fries. Drink *wa doushiyou*?" I joked, "Cheddar Coke?", enjoying the appearance of his dormant casual side. Here was a man that used chopsticks to eat pizza during company dinners in Tokyo. He decided against the cheese on everything–too messy for driving and eating. And then he shocked us all with his native Californian-level ability to juggle a burger, fries and Coke–while driving a stick shift and playing with the radio dial!–during rush hour in L.A.:

In Tokyo, he was famous for being able to dutifully drink all night with his bosses and impressively return to work–without fail–early the next morning. And now this display in L.A. I couldn't help but admire the range he had to be able to pull both of these things off.

14

The Gulf of Manners

WORKING AS A FOREIGNER in a Japanese company in Japan obliges you to serve in any number of other extra, way off-the-job-description roles that serve your more senior bosses: there's the already-mentioned roles of free English teacher, dinner honey trap double agent for foreign guests and manner buffer on overseas trips, and here's another: a diversion to ease Japanese-Korean national tensions.

Any number of cultural landmines can set off a bitter misunderstanding between Korean and Japanese businessmen, especially when they're over a certain age. You read about the historical reasons for the hard feelings, but from what I've seen, it's just as often due to a clash of manners. On one side, there's the ultra-conservative, slow and measured Japanese approach, and on the other is that prized virtue of Korean business: speed. One time, at my previous company here in Tokyo, my middle-aged Japanese boss managed to set off a new Korean customer in every possible way, all at once. And I was inserted into the affair solely because I was seen by him as a politically neutral buffer that could ease the cultural tension.

On a basic level, my boss was having trouble understanding the rapid-fire English of the Korean company's director of purchasing during conference calls, but that was far from his biggest problem. It was the way the Korean–gasp!–demanded simple, direct answers to his questions, as well as his taste for cutting-off standard-issue Japanese fence-sitting with loud, sudden confrontations. It was all so utterly un-Japanese, and my manager couldn't stand it. After these brutal calls would end, he'd often cap it with an annoyed "Tsk! *Tekitou!*", a word that, in inscrutable Japanese fashion, can inexplicably mean either "*proper*" or "*irresponsible*" (the latter clearly applying here). (It all reminded me of an interesting fact: in Japan the expression *"A rolling stone gathers no moss"* actually has a *negative* meaning: it means you cannot gain wisdom if you move around too much. In other words, moss is a good thing.).

Of course, part of my company's problem was the shaky foundation for our Korean business relationship to begin with. During the initial bid process, our company was far too slow in delivering a quotation to them, so we lost the business, with the Korean purchasing guy swearing us off for being too unresponsive to work with. This time, our typically slow reaction time even continued post-mortem. Due to somebody not CCing somebody, our slow-motion quote preparation sadly continued, despite the deal being already dead.

But then, suddenly and unexpectedly, a week later, the Korean company changed its mind, offering us another opportunity. Blind luck allowed us to use the now-completed *previous* quote. We then won the new race because we appeared to be "first", when in reality we'd not only been last, but had been lapped. This dubious victory would foreshadow everything that followed.

Now the plan was to fly to Korea, with my boss insisting I go too: "They just don't want to see a Japanese face over there, nothing'll get done. They want to see a native white-man face." He started off our first meeting in Korea with some of that stilted yet charming Japanese meeting small talk. Nervous that our dubious victory would be discovered, he let the small talk linger too long. I could see the Korean purchasing manager fidget with his fingers, cross his arms and then glare at me. It was not having the intended softening effect; he wanted the meeting to start five minutes ago. Things then went downhill fast.

My boss offered innocently: "You should visit our factory next you come Japan. It very near Sea of Japan coast, very delicious crab meat there."

Korean purchasing manager: "It not *SEA OF JAPAN*! It name is *EAST SEA!!*" Somehow, we innocently tripped the political landmine about the correct name of the strait that separates Japan's north coast and Korea.

I don't remember how we got the meeting started after that, but we did and managed to even convince the guy and his assistant to join us for the traditional sales dinner and drinks, and even set up a round of golf for all of us the next morning. After the meeting snafu, at dinner I decided I'd steer the conversation as much as possible. As the Hite beer started flowing, I felt some of the meeting tensions relax, and I pounced. As I filled our Korean supplier's glass, I teased them with my American melting pot wisdom: "Imagine if you weren't separated by the Japan, East Sea or whatever the hell you call it, and had to live together!"

But the next morning, as we teed up on the first hole, the *tekitou* problem quickly reared its head again. My boss, in the same overly earnest-looking manner our Tokyo office did its mandatory group calisthenics every morning, started to stretch to prepare for his shot. It took him a couple of minutes, and our Korean customer sat there stewing impatiently:

He then did this same stretching routine on every tee shot, just like Ichiro's famous batter's box knee bends before each at-bat. I probably shanked half my shots worrying about these two guys. On the 13th hole, the Korean casually cracked open a beer right before his tee shot. My Japanese boss raised his eyebrows at the sight of him striding lazily over, putting the beer down and teeing off without any practice swings.

The round seemed to be heading toward a calm, merciful ending after we putted out on the 18th hole. Suddenly, I looked down and saw that one of the golfers that had been a hole ahead of us had forgotten one of his irons on the green, and I picked it up. Right away he came back for it, walking right up to me and snatching it without stopping or saying "thanks", giving only a cursory nod. I didn't think too much of it, but then heard my Japanese boss scoff loudly at such a display of brusque manners: *"Mata tekitou na! (irresponsible again!)."*

Our Korean customer, mellowed by now, smiled at this. He then asked me what *tekitou* meant. I fidgeted diplomatically, and told him, "*proper*".

PART III
SALARYMAN HEALTHCARE

15

Mitamacare

THE DRINKING, TRAVEL AND GENERAL OVERWORK of the salaryman lifestyle naturally lead to anxious anticipation of the Japanese company's annual employee health exam. And one of the classic salaryman ways to try to "pass" a health exam is to stop drinking alcohol for the week before the exam.

This annual alcohol fasting pastime is standard salaryman thinking, and I'd hear guys sigh sadly to each other when saying an upcoming health check was the reason for them declining a drinking invitation. The tone of it often had the such-is-life juxtaposition and seasonal reference of a good *haiku* poem:

> *I've stopped drinking… until after my health check-up.*

But for me, my anxiety came down to surviving the Japanese universal health care exam itself, which is a gauntlet of discomfort that I've nicknamed *Mitamacare*. The exam's design, like most systems the immigrant must assimilate to here, is—in a vacuum—brilliant. But, the ability of an untrained, non-native outsider to fit into the system is doubtful at best.

Mitama is a word that literally means "honorable spirit of dead person". It's part of the Japanese tradition of worshipping ancestors–like a kind of spiritual health care for the dead. I decided on the nickname after one of my Mitamacare exams completely rocked me, even when it was showering me with amazing little medical luxuries.

I'll get into the exam experience, but first a little background. In group-fixated Japan, most company employees don't take their exam individually at their doctor's office at their own convenience (it'd take a whole book to fully explain why). Instead, most employees do it together at the same time on the same day, once a year *inside their office*. To an American, it all seems eerily Soviet, yet with the saving grace of Japanese manners overseeing the whole thing.

Inevitably, a cheery group of medical staff from the country's hospitals join in the movement and mobilize their lab stations to your office, shoehorning you and your comrades–male and female together—into meeting rooms-turned-medical exam stations:

Here you all huddle together and wait around in ultra-short medical gowns, trying not to expose yourself in the merciless florescent light. You then sheepishly shuffle from medical test-to-medical test in the female gymnast-sized slippers that they give you.

I have to say the end-result of such communal modesty is awe-inspiring. On this conveyor-belt of a medical exam, you're processed and spit-out at your desk within an hour, with no time-off needed. And yet, the medical tests are far more extensive and preventative than any HMO/PPO exam I've ever had in the U.S. It really does put the U.S. to shame.

But here's the catch: from an American point of view, it requires the discipline of a Buddhist monk–or your basic Japanese upbringing—to get through a Mitamacare exam without losing your mind. And that goes double when you forget about your company medical exam day because you're a clueless Yankee unused to communism. My fiasco started when I forgot my medical exam day was scheduled on the same day as a trip I planned to our factory in far-western Japan.

I was nicely packed for my trip, but when I woke up I glanced at my daily planner and with a shock realized that I forgot the exam. I was scheduled to leave the office for the airport at 11:00am, leaving just enough time to squeeze it in. I remembered that these exams, because they're onsite at the office, require employees to hand-carry *two* stool samples themselves from their homes by train to work (for colon cancer screening, even for those in their 20s and 30s!). This requirement alone would make my improvisation difficult from the start.

Of course, all of my Japanese colleagues followed the instructions to a T and practically wrapped their stool samples in a bow and sprayed them with perfume. But there I was, hurriedly forcing one out on the way out and stuffing the sample container crudely into my briefcase with my luggage in tow. And I still owed them another one.

Next was a mid-summer, hour-long commute standing dehydrated in a jammed Tokyo commuter train–carrying luggage too mind you–with no food or liquids in my stomach, as you have to fast for the exam blood test. Arriving at the office in terrible shape, I imagined a potential scene with my boss; having to bug him for a half-day off to go the doctor's office and produce the second sample. I didn't feel equal to this scene, so I went into the exam room hopeful of a one stool-sample compromise, but expecting the worst. Such individual rule-bending may be the norm in the U.S, but it's a sin in the automated world of Mitamacare.

Sure enough, the middle-aged nurse that greeted me frowned and then, with her bureaucratic soul beaming, presented the expected scenario: I'd have to take a half-day off to finish this. "Oh for fuck's sake" was the only thing I could say in response. But as I sat their stewing for several minutes my insides began to churn hard, and after a few minutes I triumphantly walked back over to Nurse Ratched: "Hold on. I think I'll have a second one for you in a minute. Be right back." This solved the current problem, but a bigger one was lurking around the corner.

Another little Mitamacare miracle–free testing for stomach cancer for all ages!–requires drinking a pint of barium sulfate right before the stomach x-ray. I climbed into the cramped mobile x-ray truck parked outside my office for this one, and waited with several colleagues while we all grumbled.

My name was soon called, and I quickly guzzled the white barium shake, let it settle in my stomach for a few minutes, and then went to the back of the truck. There I perched myself vertically on a rotating slab of an x-ray machine, which was operated by a technician behind a glass window. He used a little joystick to spin me around wildly, almost like I was on a mechanical bull, so that the x-ray camera could take pictures inside my stomach from all angles:

A chorus of Japanese orders streamed from him as I gagged on barium stomach gas and tried not to fall off the damned thing:

"Twist half-way to the left and bend a little forward."
"Roll around 360 degrees to stir the barium around in your stomach and then face-up."
"Stop moving when I'm taking the x-ray!!"
etc., etc.,

Not understanding his orders made me take three times as long as other employees, as I often flailed away in the wrong direction and only arrived at the right position after eliminating all of the other possibilities. Finally, after 20 minutes of this, he got the stomach x-rays from all the needed angles and it was over.

Exhausted, I carelessly drank down the little packet of pills offered to me on the way out. With a two-hour flight and a long, rural bus ride in my immediate future, I should've been focused on locking-down the explosive situation brewing in my bowels. When it was too late, I asked the nurse what those pills were that I just took. I prayed it was the Japanese equivalent of Imodium AD and not a laxative, but didn't understand the Japanese name of the medicine she said. Thinking about my trip, I then fell into a panic, and desperately mimed my situation in simple English. I pointed at my lower abdomen, and made a motion with my hands that implied "keeping my shit inside", and asked in English, "It's 'in-in', right?" Then with a down-pushing motion and a shake of my head, I added: "Not 'out-out', right?"

She seemed pleased to play this little English game, and her face beamed as she mimed back at me with her hands pushing down furiously on her abdomen: "No! Out-out! Out-out!" This is how I learned that the Mitamacare laxative is specially designed for office workers to turbo-charge the barium out of their systems in the office bathrooms while they work the rest of the day.

But I had a flight to catch, and I'd pay dearly for my mistake. I enjoyed a flight from hell that afternoon, with the final blow being a long, clenched ride on a bathroom-less rural highway bus. And then to top it off, or bottom it off, the barium-laxative cocktail didn't work as efficiently as advertised. It rocked my insides silly for days afterward. No doubt it was duking it out with the American DNA in me that feels it must shoot socialized medicine on site. During those long, boring hours afterward on the toilet, I had plenty of time to debate if this obviously superior health exam system would ever fly in the U.S. I'm a bit ashamed to say that I literally couldn't stomach the loss of personal freedom and comfort, health benefits be damned. So much so that at times I even found myself longing for my old, wretched American HMO.

At the center of my Mitamacare experience was a boxing match between conflicting values, my American neediness for personal freedom and my health, and it was a split-decision. My health won on points, just barely pulling through the moments where my sanity had me on the ropes.

16

My Colonoscopy Vacation

As a general rule, a salaryman never takes more than two consecutive days off from work unless they're really sick. It doesn't look good, and even at the progressive Japanese companies that offer flextime, employees see lots of raised eyebrows when they actually use it, as the following winning *haiku* from Dai-Ichi Life's annual Salaryman Senryu poetry contest illustrates:

> **フレックス 届け出しても 何故遅い: Even though I've given them flextime notice, "Why's he late?"**

One time, I thought I'd found a solid loophole in this Japanese workaholic, non-long-holiday-taking code: a colonoscopy. For the exam preparation, I saw myself loafing on my sofa all week, with my office's full sympathies to boot. I'd sip on a laxative while I worked through my DVR recordings, and then take trips to the commode, where I'd read peacefully:

I knew I was playing with karma, but was that desperate for some extended time off. I also had a nagging worry over some family medical history. So I signed up for the Big C despite still being well within my thirties. The first order of business was a pre-consultation with the endoscopist. And from here, my colonoscopy vacation plans began to unravel. I'd done enough research with family and other sources to know I was very likely going to be in the clear. But this Japanese doctor did none of the placating my optimistic, yet fragile American psyche begs for in such a situation.

THE SALARYMAN

I think–as George Costanza in *Seinfeld* once declared–that all doctors should have "Cancer?! Get outta here, it's just a test!" as required vocabulary for these pre-consultations. The doctor read my family history in my file, frowned and let out the Japanese equivalent of a vague, "hmm."

"Sorry, but well... what!?", I demanded, annoyed at having to introduce standard issue Japanese pessimism into a case I badly wanted to consider already closed. He then gave me an unsettling "let's see and talk afterward" kind of spiel.

Later that day, I got the hospital's colonoscopy instruction booklet in the mail. Its contents crushed my rest holiday plans further. It explained that in ultra-efficient Japan they practice "same-day colon evacuation". The Japanese pharmaceutical industry, no doubt spurred on by the same workaholic, no-holiday code as my company, has apparently lapped the world on laxative technology. So there'd be no comfy "prep" days off beforehand like in the U.S, and I'd come to know what Japanese colonoscopy prep is: an intense, nuclear laxative-fueled, communal toilet orgy done within a few hours at a hospital.

When I got there that day, I was promptly placed in the preparation room with a dozen or so other patients there for the same thing. I was the only one there not collecting a pension, and, of course, the only non-Japanese. I stared self-consciously at my one-gallon bottle of milky-white laxative. A couple of retired salarymen soon sidled up with their own bottles and began chatting with me. One of them tilted his bottle with a mock "*Kanpai!*" (cheers!), and we poured ourselves the first of many nasty rounds.

My mood began to shift as I felt the polite, disarming Japanese charm begin to work its magic on me again, as it has often done in other laughably uncomfortable foreigner situations. On the waiting room TV, a nurse put on a short Japanese animation that depicted a colonoscopy procedure. It made the whole thing seem cute and benign, almost whimsical. "Now don't worry at all or be embarrassed", chirped the cartoon doctor.

Starting to really percolate inside but feeling surprisingly at ease, I hit the commode–again and again. I'll spare you the graphic details, but picture Mt. Fuji erupting and you'd have a good idea of what was happening in those hospital bathrooms.

And here is where the famous charm of Japanese toilets were a godsend. This is a device so lovingly designed that it effectively countered the strain of all that nuclear laxation. The soft, heated seats. The way its washlet menu housed countless controls to play with–like nozzle angle, stream power and an addictive pulsating mode– making the experience a borderline pleasure each time. And the way it had a button that played the sounds of a waterfall on an invisible toilet speaker, designed specifically to drown-out the embarrassing noise of your laxative-induced explosions. I half-expected to find a button that said "colon massage", right next to the one for "grenade launcher".

The super-lax cocktail rampaged on inside me and the toilet trips continued. I distracted myself from the task at hand by dreaming up a business plan for exporting these Japanese toilets. The medicine was working so well now that my mind began to race ahead. How on Earth would it be possible to suddenly make the abrupt transition from my current explosive state to that of a non-spurting patient on the operating table? The thought of my Mt. Fuji erupting rudely onto my doctor at that crucial insertion moment seemed very possible.

I couldn't bear this thought, so I asked the nurse about it privately as I nervously undressed for the procedure. She waved me off with a smile as she prepared for game time: "Nobody's had that problem before, but then again you're the first foreigner we've had."

Her comment didn't help, so I took a quick stroll at the last minute to try to ease my mind. At the end of the hall, I came upon the staff room door. It suddenly opened and inside I saw what to me looked like a few endoscopists doing what looked like group calisthenics. This was a very traditional Japanese morning group warm-up ritual that I'd seen practiced before in various places, mostly in the early morning with laborers at factories or blue-collar guys at construction sites. A misgiving came over me: this procedure is so intense that they need to warm-up first? As the door closed, I shuddered. I could just see them in there doing practice arm thrusts to prepare for jamming in the colon scope.

But thanks to the drugs it was all over before I knew it. I soon awoke in a post-op haze to my endoscopist hovering over me and assuring me in halting English, "You OK. Nice pink colon."

In the recovery room I and several other patients tried to stifle what felt like a Hummer-tank load of trapped intestinal gas. Alas, there were no buttons as on the Japanese toilet to play a melody to cover up the noises leaking from us. But by that point I was so relieved–and ready to return to the office after my colonoscopy "getaway"–that it hardly mattered.

17

Samurai Orthopedic Surgeon

IF YOU'RE THE TYPICAL train-commuting salaryman in Tokyo who walks two-plus miles a day, even a minor leg injury will descend you into something that belongs in Dante's Nine Circles of Hell. When you roll an ankle, or blow out a knee playing basketball as I did, the wonderful cafes, chair massages and bars that buffer your stifling Tokyo grind instantly fade from your daily menu.

Walking on crutches, you don't dare stray from the straight-line course that gets you to the office and back in one piece each day. It takes all you've got to handle the wicked obstacle course that Tokyo becomes without two good wheels under you.

First off, using crutches to walk around Tokyo all day quickly turns your hands numb and arms achy. So instead of cocktails and fun, you spend your nights mapping out new train routes to the office that slice minutes off your walking time (Tokyo is brilliant that way–there's always several sneaky options for getting to the same place). And on the trains each day, you pray that one of the exhausted salarymen sleeping in the handicap seats wakes up, notices you and gives up his seat.

Sometimes this happens, but when it doesn't, you have to stand and balance yourself on one leg, like a flamingo, and sway on your crutches for the 60 minutes it takes to get to your station, too afraid to scratch an itch on your nose lest you fall down. If you do snag a seat, your hurt leg sticks out straight into the aisle and parts the mass of commuting humanity.

Your head is on a swivel as you identify various threats to your knee: the older salaryman in front of you on your left who is so exhausted that he snores while standing, the 90 pound middle-aged office lady who's been smooshed by the crowd and dangles dangerously over your legs, the young schoolboy straddling your feet carelessly with his head buried in a video game player. You have to pop up using your one good leg and stand up in front of your seat to get your protruding limb out of their way at every stop so they don't fall over it. This routine happens 20 times as you take the local train to your destination: sit 5 minutes-pop up 1 minute, sit 5 minutes-pop up 1 minute, etc. When you finally get to your connecting station, you then discover that you badly miscalculated in your planning the night before, as a 50-step stairway awaits you.

Still, I had some degree of control over these post-operation, daily commuting disasters. And I found an excellent way to deal with my train hell: I invented a discrete, in-train cocktail—I named my Tokyo hip flask "the Sadsack"—that mixes 50-proof *shochu* (distilled liquor from barley) with a canned, carbonated cocktail of lemon Chu-HI. The plain water bottle you pour this into ensures nobody knows that you're Sadsacking your way home (this also is further proof of my theory that Tokyo has a perfect consumer antidote for each and every one of a commuter's stresses):

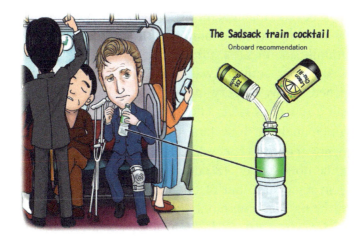

The Tokyo trains were one thing, but I was lucky I'd gotten that far, as my built-in language handicap actually presented far more danger during my pre-surgery doctor visits and during my hospital stay.

At my first visit with my knee surgeon, he pronounced in rapid-fire Japanese without blinking that my knee's meniscus was torn but could be stitched up and repaired. This much I thought I followed, and it was a great relief. I wanted no part of having a big chunk of it removed–a.k.a "meniscectomy"–and the increased risk of having to limp around like Fred Sanford later in life. As I tend to do when high-level Japanese conversations flow out of my range, my mind began to wander as he kept talking. I started to notice there was a robotic precision to his movements as he talked, his head bobbing up-and-down and side-to-side in perfect unison with the subtle movement of his svelte hands. To a clumsy and fat-fingered American guy like me, it suggested the famous manual dexterity and precision manufacturing of the Japanese. I thought I was lucky to have hurt myself in a land of such naturally coordinated surgeons.

But this comfort was knocked to ruins when I opened up my surgery instruction guide that came by mail a few days later. The name of my procedure was written in large font Japanese on the top: 半月切除 (meniscectomy). I wondered if when I'd spaced out, did he do a sudden 180 degree turn, as in, "I'd like to try to repair it… but of course, etc. etc."? Or was he just being non-committal about it until he opened me up? Or worse yet, as I dreamed later that night, did I make some stupid Japanese paperwork error at the hospital and sign up for a meniscus chop job? I saw that one of the Japanese kanji used to spell meniscectomy contained a symbol…

… that literally means "cut out". And since the right symbol of this Japanese character literally means "sword", and is meant to resemble the shape of a blade, it also has other several violent meanings. Realizing this chilled my spine.

As I slept that night, my imagination ran wild. In my nightmare, my paperwork error was irreversible, and a samurai orthopedic surgeon took aim at my meniscus on the operating table:

Of course, it was all just a nurse's clerical error, and it was quickly cleared up. My focus soon became not on the surgery itself, but on the comforts of my 7-DAY HOSPITAL STAY after surgery. This is a perk of Japanese universal health care, but the stay was sprinkled with danger thanks to my foreignness.

Past knee surgery experience in the U.S. had taught me to avoid the post-op bladder catheter if at all possible. Land of blessed manual dexterity be damned, the horrible 60 seconds of nurse catheter tube insertion was not something I ever wanted to experience again. I asked the head nurse, and she not only first refused me on the grounds of hospital rules, but told me I'd have to keep a catheter in for a WHOLE NIGHT AND DAY after surgery to prevent messes (the rules, I learned, were designed for their typical patient: a disabled 70-something-year old Japanese man). She lectured me that since I was sharing a recovery room with six other elderly patients, all following this rule, I MUST obey the rule like them.

But my Samurai Surgeon was on my side when I escalated the discussion to him, and she settled the catheter debate by giving me a little, bedside pitcher-like thing to relieve myself in when I needed (while also giving me my first free market victory vs. Japanese socialized Mitamacare. But I still bore a social cost: the whole room no doubt could hear every drop coming from me whenever I went as our beds were only separated by a thin curtain, and a couple of times I had a pop-in nurse visit in the middle of taking care of my business).

So I won on this one, but only because I'd carefully prepared myself for the catheter debate by researching in advance all of the Japanese vocabulary I'd need to use. From there on out, I'd have to improvise my Japanese in the face of trouble...a dangerous game for a foreigner to play in a hospital.

Things got hairy pretty quickly. Before surgery, I hadn't realized that I set off alarms with my anesthesiologist when discussing my asthma. His eyes widened when I showed him my American inhaler, and this apparently trumped my unclear explanation about how truly mild my asthma was. My Japanese gibberish and the alien prescription totally spooked him. So behind the scenes he directed my nurses to cut me off from all the normal post-surgery, pain-killing meds in an apparent ultra-conservative attempt to prevent some imagined asthma attack induced by...I don't know. Induced by my comfort at being relieved from great pain, I guess. His attention to safety I suppose was laudable, and otherwise the attention of the Japanese nurses was really beyond what you'd ever see in the U.S., but I forgot all this the morning after my surgery. When I found out why normal pain meds hadn't been given to me all night, I yelled in English, "Forget the asthma, PLEASE! This fucking thing has been killing me all night!" That quickly righted things.

Then a couple of days later, when I developed a high fever from an infection in my arm from the IV tube, a nurse explained that she had to quickly deliver a fever-reducer to me in a non-IV way. She told me to roll over, and from what I grasped, she'd inject something "on" my butt. As I bared by bottom, her hands probed much deeper than I expected, and, within a millisecond, the Eagle had landed. I had myself a Chevy Chase-meets-proctologist moment from *Fletch* as I yelled, "Oh! You meant IN, not 'on'!"

PART IV
ADVANCED TOPICS

18

Reverse Culture Shock

EVER SINCE I BECAME A SALARYMAN, I've had a fantasy of being transferred by my Japanese company back to the US as an expatriate. With American big-city housing, car and healthcare costs all fully subsidized by the company, the U.S. loses a lot of its frontier roughness that sometimes scares you back into Japan's safer, softer bosom.

At least that's what I thought when I once got transferred to San Jose for a few months by my company. You see, a Japanese salaryman transferred overseas without his family basically takes it as a rest cure from the real-life Japan grind. Don't get me wrong, they miss their families as most anyone would, but personally I've witnessed too many jailbreak reactions from them as they realize they're free from headquarters office bureaucracy and all those heavy rules, and, of course, Manner Mode.

The Japanese in my San Jose office utterly soaked in the California lifestyle, and the rest-cure reputation I'd heard of their expat life fed my fantasy. But I found that after living for so long in Japan, I'd become a pseudo-foreigner in my home country, and that tempered my enjoyment of these reverse expat perks. It was the backlash of overseas wanderlust, as I realized that I was now a fish out of water in *both* countries: the place where I immigrated to, and now, *the place where I'm from too.*

I dealt with several reverse culture shocks as I got re-acquainted with domestic American life at my furnished one-bedroom California apartment:

Reverse Culture Shock #1: Clothes Dryers

The washer/dryer unit that was included in my apartment felt foreign to me. Because of cultural reasons that'd take a book to fully explain, standalone dryers don't exist in Japanese houses, let alone in apartments. Basically, due to a lack of space, dryers in Japan only come built-in as a dual-function within the washer. And it's an expensive, high-end option.

Still, even the people who own these basically just ignore the dryer. This is because all Japanese feel they *MUST* hang their washed, wet clothes outside every morning to air-dry. This selfless act of energy-saving drudgery is an essential part of being a good Japanese, and always has been. Japanese society expects everyone to do it: housewives, the super-rich, fugitives on the lam. If you don't do it, your neighbors will quickly notice and start to whisper about it, and their sidelong glances will come to torture you.

Heeding to this mindset is why having my own personal dryer during my U.S. stay threatened my cultural identity. I forgot that blasting my wet clothes with 40 minutes of raw American power was my Constitutional birthright! I loved it, but the thing about it was... Japan had ruined it for me. I just couldn't enjoy pigging out on electricity like I used to. And another drawback of all that power is the other wastage. Yes, I'm talking about that other standard feature of American dryers: their magical ability to lose your socks.

After my first wash load in my San Jose place, I took my clothes out of the dryer to find that one of my new business socks had disappeared without a trace in there. And a gray and mysterious newborn baby sock had suddenly appeared in its place. This is further proof that all American dryers are connected to a space wormhole that transports your lost socks to a world called "SockLand":

Reverse Culture Shock #2: Americans ranting at bad customer service

When I first got to Japan, it took some time to get used to store clerks actually caring about their jobs and customer service actually working like it was supposed to. I think it's because Japan has removed tipping from the whole equation, and as a result has de-socialized a lot of the consumer experience. Japan fills the social retail void with things like toilets that tickle your bottom, and supermarket doors that yell out *irashaimase!* ("Welcome!"):

THE SALARYMAN

There's a casual, social component to customer service in the US that's charming to come home to after getting used to Japan. You really miss the frustrated, funny rants you hear people go on when dealing with bad American customer service. There's a sizable segment of Americans, including my dad, who – customer service or perhaps some technology product failing them – are satisfied enough if they like the person they are dealing with, or at the least that person lets them vent. Japan's vastly superior service – if you want to nitpick – does feel too automated at times, leaving my American palate hungry for some of that personal ranting with store clerks or telephone support agents that I grew up with.

I saw this bad service-equalized-by-socializing exchange throughout my childhood, most vividly at the barbershop my dad went to for years. A friendly Italian barber there named Alberto would massacre his hair every two months, with my dad and him talking excitedly throughout the butchering, my dad not even noticing what was happening (nor noticing my brother and I either in the waiting area, where we were usually looking at a *Playboy* that we'd hidden inside of the *Sports Illustrated* we were holding, the magazines being another social equalizer of this barber).

It proves a cross-cultural point to me now: a funny, social personality – not obedience and polite manners as you see in Japan – almost always overcomes a lot of flaws in the U.S. It's well-known that to be merely likable and funny can make you a good American salesman, and good at customer service, but I see now that American consumers also use these traits to deal with their frustration at erratic, inattentive American service.

Nowhere was the socializing of the whole consumption experience more necessary than in my dad's old home office, where I saw some nasty personal battles with technology over the years. First, it was the PC in the early 90s that turned his office upside down. With its insidious software and email, it broke down his old pillars: the phone, the file and the face-to-face talk.

As a teenager in those days, I'd be in his office collating papers for him, with him usually hunched over the hated computer. The White Sox game would be on the radio to temper my boredom, and distract him between his periodic rages at his PC (one of which was so bad that he renamed his desktop folders 'fuck', 'shit' and as many other curse words he could think of).

It's been a never-ending uphill climb for him ever since, like Camus' mountain of absurdity. Only my dad plays the mythical Greek Sisyphus: eternally motivated to push his technology projects up a hill only to see them roll back down at him each time as a wad of error pop-ups, tangled cables and useless technical support.

By the time I was sent to San Jose on my 3-month hiatus from Japan, his two-decade-plus battle with his PC was basically over. (Though the war still raged on in his head: on his latest Bucket List is dropping his laptop out of his future nursing home's top floor window).The battleground had moved to his smartphone and the messy business of using all those irresistible apps. The ever-important account password was now his personal bane in this new smartphone order: creating them, writing them down, finding them. And add to that the frustrating reality of modern technology life: the stronger your password is – those damn "your password isn't strong enough" error messages seem to be appearing more and more each year – the more likely it is that you'll forget it.

During my time back in the U.S. I visited my parent's home in Chicago, and remember finding my dad in his old office on the speaker phone with technical support once again, his frustration loud enough to hear from the kitchen. This time he was trying to figure out why his beloved satellite radio smartphone app had stopped working. (Side note: he listens to exactly ONE radio station on this satellite radio service that offers around 20,000 stations – the one that plays his favorite old Hollywood film scores from the 1950s). It all came down to an account password the fussy app suddenly refused to accept. I started to overhear the conversation when it had already reached its breaking point, after he and tech support had been struggling with the password for some time:

DAD: Your logic, uh, I don't follow that. OK, all right, I'll enter, give me, uh, anything. YOU make it up.

TECH SUPPORT GUY: Well I can't make your password up. For security, YOU have to make that up.

DAD: Well why not, what could happen? Jesus, you could log-in and listen to my radio! *(frustrated laugh)* And you'd have to listen to my music that's 70 years outdated! God, that would be the end! You wouldn't want that to happen!

TECH SUPPORT GUY: No, not at all.

DAD: OK, so I'm supposed to enter a new password that I'll forget, or that it won't recognize after I write it down.

TECH SUPPORT GUY: You need to use one capital letter and one number.

DAD: All right, OK. Let me try this. *(one minute delay)* Well I have to change it to something completely new. I'll just make something up, one that I'll forget. Or that this system won't accept even if I remember it anyway.

TECH SUPPORT GUY: Hopefully, it does.

DAD: Well, that's what I said before, obviously it didn't.

TECH SUPPORT GUY: Maybe you just forgot it. (Author's note: hearing such a direct comment from customer support sent a small shock wave through me when I heard it, as it's impossible to imagine a Japanese agent speaking to a customer this way)

DAD: *(annoyed)* No, I wrote it down. And I use it for everything else too. Jesus, next time I'm going to put it on the blimp that flies over Wrigley Field so I don't lose it!

TECH SUPPORT GUY *(sighing)* Gotcha.

DAD: Oh, it's asking me for my user name. I don't know the password to enter now, frankly.

TECH SUPPORT GUY: You want to put the password in that you just made up.

DAD: "Does not match our records", it says.

TECH SUPPORT GUY: OK, we need to re-register your account, so you need to go click that icon at the top right, and you need to re-register. And not just change the password.

DAD: OK, well, I thought we'd done that.

TECH SUPPORT GUY: Yeah, I thought so also.

DAD: OK, I'm back to the "access my account part".and it has my username already typed in. And now for the password, I have no idea.

TECH SUPPORT GUY: It should have a link that says "forgot password". Click on that.

DAD: Even though I wrote it down *(frustrated laugh)*.

TECH SUPPORT GUY: Right. So, go ahead and put in… what is it asking you now?

DAD: It's asking me, uh, "identify your account". I gotta put in my username, I guess.

TECH SUPPORT GUY: Yeah, that is *(gives email address)*.

DAD: And that's all in lowercase?

TECH SUPPORT GUY: Yes, all in lowercase.

DAD: I pushed "done". *(speaking to himself)* Hmm, "continue". "We do not find your username in our records". Oh wait, I left a "C" out. *(slight delay)* Now it says, "we don't have you in our records", and I typed it in correctly this time. I am still alive, am I not? Or am I imagining I'm still alive? *(frustrated laugh)*

TECH SUPPORT GUY: So you typed in T as in Tango, A as in … *(spells out username)*.

DAD: Let me go back and put a capital on the first T, see if that helps.

TECH SUPPORT GUY: No, don't do that. There's no capital in it.

DAD: Well, that's what I have written down, and this doesn't work anyway. So, why not?

TECH SUPPORT GUY: OK, if you have any issues, um, what I'm going to do is, transfer you, maybe in accounts, um, they have some advanced technical support, what I'll do is transfer you and you'll soon get a confirmation of this support ticket at your email, that is….

DAD: Hold it, Hold it, Hold it. I got… I got, "what is my favorite pet's name?" It went right to that.

TECH SUPPORT GUY: OK, go ahead and put that information in.

DAD: Besides, I like talking to you. I might not like the next person.

TECH SUPPORT GUY: Oh, that's OK.

DAD: My question is how did I lose this to begin with?

TECH SUPPORT GUY: I'm not sure.

DAD: Well, that's what they said the last time it happened.

TECH SUPPORT GUY: *(Laughing)*

DAD: Well let me try this… we've had so many pets. I forgot which one I used. Let me try another pet. *(types it in)* Nope, that doesn't work. *(1 minute delay) (frustrated)* You know I'm not trying to access somebody's savings account, you know? I'm trying to turn on a goddamn radio! *(frustrated laugh)* Jee-sus Christ. Whoever designed this system, can you give them my regards, would you? Suggestions on what they can do with it, where they can stick it.

TECH SUPPORT: *(laughter)*

DAD: *(reading next account security question)* "What was my first phone number?" *(frustrated laugh)*. God! My first phone number? You probably can't remember yours and you're only like 25 years old right?!

TECH SUPPORT GUY: I probably couldn't.

DAD: Is all this security really necessary? What could happen? Somebody else could tie-in and listen to my crap, right?

TECH SUPPORT GUY: *(laughter)*

DAD: That's the worst thing that can happen that I can think of!

TECH SUPPORT GUY: Right.

DAD: The security questions…. my answers don't match. It says try again.

TECH SUPPORT GUY: Yeah see you gotta re-register.

DAD: I thought that's what we started…

TECH SUPPORT GUY: We gotta find out why your account is not working and for that we gotta get you transferred, OK?

DAD: Thanks for your help.

TECH SUPPORT GUY: Oh no problem.

DAD: No problem to you; it's a problem to ME.

TECH SUPPORT GUY: Will get this taken care of for you.

DAD: I wanna do something else today, OK?

TECH SUPPORT GUY: I gotcha. Anything else I can do for you?

DAD: No, thanks for your patience.

[on hold for 5 minutes, then new tech support answers the line]

DAD: Hello, my app on my phone, it's the second time it's disappeared. It doesn't recognize any of the information I put in, and I can't change, and um, I've tried two ways. I tried to reload it from the app store, and it doesn't recognize my Apple ID, and then I tried to register it using my user name and password from your site, and that didn't seem to work either. That's the reason I'm always having to change them, because the old ones don't work! *(frustrated laugh)* And I'm very proud of myself when I write them down somewhere, and I'm not trying to access anybody's saving account. I'm trying to turn on a God damned radio that I already paid for, all right?

TECH SUPPORT GUY #2: OK, sir…

DAD: And I haven't been able to log on to this for a week, so I haven't had time to screw around with it.

TECH SUPPORT GUY #2: *(blandly)* Am I to understand you are having trouble with the app on your phone?

DAD: Yes.

TECH SUPPORT GUY #2: Let me first ask you some questions so I can pull up your account here.

DAD: The guy that I talked to before can't pass that information on to you? We have to go through this process all over again is what you're telling me? I want to make PROGRESS, not REGRESS. All right, we got that straight?

MOM *(overhearing from the kitchen and yelling out):* Tom! Be respectful!

DAD: Are you there? Hello?… Hello? ….

. . .

All-in-all, the conversation was a good reminder of how funny and casually social the customer service experience in the US can be.

Reverse Culture Shock #3: Garbage duties

In the US, I experienced a guilty pleasure at being unchained from my exhausting, ecological, taking-out-the-garbage duties in Japan. In Japan, you spend 10 minutes almost every early morning carefully separating my burnable trash from the unburnables. In a rush to make my morning Tokyo train, I have to squash our perfectly-tied little garbage bags with my foot to make them fit into the tiny, cute, standard Japanese-sized garbage can.

Or on the days I have many unburnable garbage bags, I must stack them symmetrically so our trash looks presentable to the Tokyo neighborhood. In the U.S., I simply stuffed my trash into any big, untied bag I want, whenever I felt like it. I then tossed it carelessly over my head and into one of those vast steel dumpsters on my way to my gas-guzzling SUV rental. I must shamefully admit that, like most Americans, I only like the *idea* of being ecological. But *being* ecological? Well, geez... I mean, only if other people, like, see it and give me extra credit for it.

In Japan, good ecology is already built-into daily life. People just don't make a big deal out of it or complain about recycling like they do in the U.S. Of course, this is the way it should be, but it just won't do here. It's because good ecology takes work. And while work and self-sacrifice are the national religion in Japan, I realized that we Americans need a little Scooby Snack for our effort.

Reverse Culture Shock #4: American Toilets

Which leads me to the confusing and downright primitive toilet situation in the U.S. In public bathrooms, it's downright scary what a grown American man will do behind the closed doors of a stall. It doesn't matter if you're at an art exposition, a fancy country club wedding reception, or a Hollywood movie premier. You're cringing whenever you open that stall door in the U.S. And besides the primitive toilet manners of us American men, with all the squawking these days about smart devices, green energy etc. etc. – how does the entire S&P 500 just leave the US saddled with Soviet industrial design, mass-of-toilet paper needing, cold-seated toilet technology?

And how can a society that salivates over every new iPhone release neglect such a basic and... ahem... *bottom*-line need? Maybe Apple needs to come out with an iToilet to civilize the American bathroom. Because people need to be fired at Toto, Japan's leading toilet maker, for somehow failing to unleash their amazing electronic seat, bidet Washlet toilet on the blatantly needy American market. (if you think I'm exaggerating: according to Wikipedia, 72% of Japanese homes now have Washlets, and they're standard issue now in most *PUBLIC* bathrooms, which means a homeless Japanese person enjoys more toilet luxury than an American billionaire).

This is a device so lovingly designed and rewarding that I promise you it'll become like another family member to you, as it has for me. Not only is the Washlet ecologically superior – it all but makes toilet paper obsolete – but its long list of perks, some of which I already mentioned during my colonoscopy story, are universal: There's the soft, heated electronic seat…. The way the washlet menu houses countless controls to customize, like nozzle angle, stream force, water temperature and, my favorite, the "pulsating" mode… And the way its motion-activated auto-cleaning spray prepares a lovely, misty morning toilet bowl for you first thing in the morning.

I imagine Toto's engineers are at work building the next generation of Japanese washlet toilets, featuring an animated water stream that takes the form of a human hand and reaches in gently and snatches the poop from inside you, saving you from the effort:

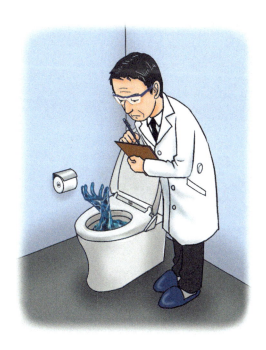

All you need to know is that Google is a believer. Reportedly, the bathrooms at its famous, cutting-edge Mountain View headquarters are stocked with Japanese washlets.

So get ready, the signs point to a coming global digital toilet invasion. America, I beg you: Give Japanese toilets a chance.

19

Hello Work!

I WAS ONCE UNEMPLOYED for a few months in Japan when I was in-between jobs. The experience taught me the true social value of having a job here, and I learned, the hard way, why working is Japan's true national religion. To start with, obviously I'm no natural-born, workaholic Japanese salaryman. In fact, when I was a lad in the U.S., I had a knack for avoiding work. My dad always griped that I was a master at it, a real natural. So it was that at the start I had a silly, dreamy American idea of what my jobless months in Japan would be like.

I imagined it'd be terrifying, but in a heroic kind of way. I saw the fear inspiring great bursts of energy that'd carry me to some un-imagined career path. Instead, unemployment in Japan was merely dull and humbling, its subtle little humiliations pounding me into a funk that I was lucky to escape. I'd start the days by opening my eyes in bed before 6:00am, and then lie there for half an hour, too inert to face the silence of my email inbox. (As a foreigner in Japan, your batting average for getting a response for a job application is exponentially lower than that of a Japanese: your foreign experience being far too exotic, your Japanese never fluent enough. However, when you do hear something back your closing rate is probably higher.)

One particular day early on, I got up before everyone else in the house so I could pound the cyber pavement in peace. I had a hop in my step that day, until I stopped to read a note that the garbage collection company had left for me the previous week, which I had left out as a reminder to myself on the kitchen counter. Its banality instantly punctured my breadwinning vibe: "Don't waste bags by using too many and you must tie them up right or we cannot accept them." Later that morning, as I loafed on the sofa – the picture of unshaved joblessness – my son whispered something to my baby girl that rattled me further:

Little domestic tweaks like these show how Japanese society's obsession with *mottainai* puts the squeeze on the jobless man in Japan, driving him out of the house and into an office, where he belongs.

I jumped up, shaved and dressed myself. Then I took our garbage and empty cans out, hoping to avoid my neighbors. Nothing sticks out in a Japanese neighborhood mid-morning on a weekday more than an out-of-work salaryman, especially a foreign one. And nothing gives away a change in your job status like the beer cans you put in your street's recycling bin (beer-drinking statistics are actually an official economic indicator in Japan and are often cited in newscasts).

In Japan, there are three beer categories, the best and most expensive one occupied by the famous Asahi, Sapporo, Suntory and Kirin brands. In my jobless state, there would be no guilt-free drinking done from this beloved tier. I had to indulge in the second-class category – the lower-malt, lower-cost *happoshu* ("carbonated alcohol beverage") – a fall that spoke volumes to anyone watching.

To my annoyance, my retired salaryman neighbor shuffled out with his cans at the exact same time as me. He looked down at my beer cans, studied them and – after a torturous five-second delay – commented, "*Happoshu ka. Saikin taihen dane!*" ("Ahh, happoshu is it? Things *are* tough these days, aren't they!"):

He must've known this was a touchy subject for an idle salaryman, as he didn't get into the very real possibility of me free-falling down into the third and very bottom beer tier: the ominously-named *daisan* (literally means "The Third"). I went back inside, humbled by this reminder that there's only one acceptable state of healthy adult male existence in Japan: Asahi-laced servitude to a big company.

This mindset drove me to my monthly appointments at the local office of *Hello Work*, Japan's English-named national unemployment insurance service (yes, they even try to turn the shame of unemployment into a cute thing in Japan). At the *Hello Work* office, you had to follow their purely ceremonial requirement of "applying" for their listed job openings in order to qualify for your welfare payout.

THE SALARYMAN

I entered the *Hello Work* building later that day – one of those harshly lit Japanese government offices – and sat down in a room with rows of wooden benches and several numbered counters. Dozens of other unemployed people were there – mostly Japanese men in their 40s and 50s, with a handful of older women as well.

We were all there to search through their job databases and list up the jobs we wanted to apply to (rumor had it that government-friendly companies provided the listings just to serve the purpose of this ceremonial job search requirement). Then you'd have to wait there for them to decide how many of your selected jobs you were qualified to apply to. After this, a clerk – a grumpy middle-aged man with sweaty armpits and matted-down hair growing low on his forehead – would bark out your name. He'd yell, "Mr. such and such, 20 jobs. Please come forward."

Sometimes, it was only 10 or 15 jobs, but whatever it was, the whole room knew it. After a while my name was called; its unnatural foreign sound – like a record needle scratching on vinyl – instantly drew the whole room's attention. Busy people in the room abruptly stopped what they were doing, their eyes honing in on me as the clerk called out my name and job search results: "Michael *Ha-wa-dou*-san: zero jobs."

People couldn't help laughing, but thankfully I'd learned from previous visits to sit in the front row so I didn't have to see their faces. I quickly walked up, accepted my welfare slip and walked out head-down, muttering to myself. Later, on the way home, I spotted a very successful friend in the distance walking directly toward me. I quickly dove into a pricey café to avoid him, and, of course, then had to buy something.

You could multiply all of the above disasters by a hundred; it's all part of the experience of being an unemployed foreigner in Japan. Fittingly, this dreadful period came to an end in the most random, uninspired way possible. I stumbled across a job accidentally when I emailed a former colleague about him returning a book he'd borrowed from me. He replied that his company had a job opening fit for a foreigner, so why don't I come in and talk about it?

And boom!… that's how I ended my time as a jobless man in Japan and gloriously returned to Asahi-sipping salarymanhood.

20

The Invisible Hand of the Tokyo Economy

SEVERAL YEARS INTO MY SALARYMANHOOD, I developed my own economic theory that I believe partly explains how capitalism works in Tokyo. It's a modern spin on the famous economist Adam Smith's "Invisible Hand" theory, from his 18th century treatise *The Wealth of Nations*. Smith used the hand metaphor to imply there's a moral logic to free markets, and that unchecked individual economic behavior brings unintended public benefits (a theory you hear plundered in the film *Wall Street* during Gordon Gekko's "Greed is Good" speech).

The Invisible Hand I see in Tokyo is the unintended benefits created by the unchecked individual *incompetence* of traditional Japanese corporate management. They drive their rank-and-file salarymen and female employees crazy, instilling in them a monstrous hunger for retail refreshment to deal with their pent-up frustration.

This mechanism – deflationary incompetence converted into triumphant consumption – reveals the power of the most brilliant jewel of the Japanese economy: the incredible quality, and global competitiveness, of its recession-proof retail wonderland. (I'm not sure Smith would agree with me that this proves another thing he wrote: "Consumption is the sole end and purpose of all production").

So basically, Smith's old theory predicts economic growth from *production* gains, while my theory predicts *consumption* gains that equalize the big production losses caused by terrible Tokyo managers, thereby saving the country from deep recession, not to mention showing that the true GDP value of the Japanese economy is probably underrated:

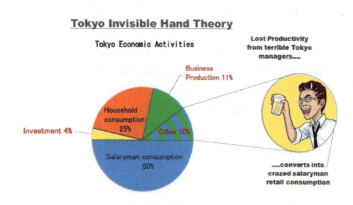

I should clarify that incompetence is no more rampant in Japanese business than anywhere else. The difference is how Japanese manners handcuff everybody from doing anything about it. People basically just put up with it. This drives my Hand Theory: the GDP void caused by a useless Tokyo manager, who cannot get fired because of Japan's lifetime employment laws, is filled back in by all the café and bar binging and night crawling needed to blow off the steam of carrying on with the charade of politely following such leadership.

To illustrate, as I originally wrote down the notes years ago that led to me writing this chapter, my ENTIRE office was sitting in a three-hour meeting to listen to EACH employee one-by-one state his or her's three goals for the next year, ignoring whether your jobs were even remotely connected. Only a big Tokyo company can waste people's time like this, and only a Tokyo salaryman quietly lets them waste it. Naturally, and providing proof that my theory works, the company held an all-you-can drink "dinner" after the meeting.

・・・

Robokoppu is the nickname of my former boss at one of my former companies, and he's an instructive case study for my Hand theory. His chief activities as a middle manager were obsessing over company rules, using them as a ceremonial tool to reconfirm his seniority, and trying to look busy. The Japanese on my team came up with *Robokoppu* (the Japanese pronunciation of the famous *Robocop* movie character) behind his back, not only because of his stickler-ways, but because of his mechanical gait and erect way of walking. His stiff bearing was accentuated by his taste for heavily starched shirts with high-collars. His jet black hair was heavily gelled and pressed down, as if he were punishing it for trying to stick out:

An unusual case, he invaded our little world from the Tokyo unemployment line–laid off from one of Japan's dying memory device makers, a totally different industry from our company. He seemed to have been randomly thrown into his position as sales director over us, not being remotely qualified to do the job of even his subordinates.

He did, however, prove expert at the Tokyo managerial art of using company rules and bureaucratic manners to compensate for incompetence. This, together with his general shiftiness, made him very difficult to deal with. My Invisible Hand theory crystalized during the experience of dealing with this man.

Five highlights from the *Robokoppu* experience, and how it inevitably converted into a net positive economic event:

(1) To look busy, he'd bring documents with him to the office urinal, hold them up and read them under his breath.

(2) To avoid the personal exposure of being in charge of establishing a new customer, and ignoring each team member's valuable familiarity with their accounts, he reshuffled our account assignments alphabetically. He assigned himself the accounts starting with the letters A-F, which contained our top three existing, and easiest to maintain, Japanese customers. When somebody pointed out that one tough, new American customer that started with a "B" was in his self-assigned range, he later announced that since the company's name started with "The", the customer would be listed as starting under the letter "T".

(3) Every morning during our 8:30am team roll call, he made us read aloud in unison two company rules from the company rulebook. He knew that I in particular hated this formality, and so one morning he took my being three minutes late to the morning roll call as a direct rebellion:

Me (arriving at 8:33am): Sorry I'm late, I had to get off my train to use the men's room.

Robokoppu: Why you no call!

Me: When? You aren't supposed to talk on the phone on trains in Japan, right? Anyway, I texted you.

Robokoppu: I don't read text before 8:30am. Rule is MUST call. You must do after you go bathroom.

Me: I didn't know if I'd actually be late then. Another train came right away and I got on it.

Robokoppu: Well, you must get off again and call and say why late.

Me: Why? Then I would've gotten here much later. I wanted to get here as fast as I could.

Robokoppu: No, late is late, most important is tell me.

Me (frustrated laugh): Sorry, but that's nutty.

Robokoppu: "*Na-chi*"?

Me: Yeah. Doesn't make sense.

Robokoppu: I your boss.

Me: What'd I miss? Two minutes of everyone repeating stupid company rules! What a crock of shit!

Robokoppu: "*Clock of sheeet*"?

(5) We had two printers in our office: one for making copies and one for printing things out (which was silly in itself). Both were leased machines, and the company paid by the page, with the copying one being like three yen (3 cents) more expensive per page than the printing one. So because of this and the underperformance of our team's sales the year he was there, he declared that anyone in our sales team that wanted to make any copies had to scan them, convert them to PDFs, and then print them out. To celebrate when he left the company, our sales team estimated how much money we had saved by following his rule (if memory serves, about 7,000 Yen, or $60). We used this savings estimate to convince our new sales director to partially treat us to a rampaging night at an *izakaya*, thus replacing our lost productivity from following the Robokoppu's rule with a consumption gain, and proving my Tokyo Invisible Hand theory once and for all.

21

The Golden Years of Salarymanhood

A FEW YEARS AGO, about eight years into becoming a salaryman, my chest hair started to turn gray. Whitish strands started to spread like dead brush into my upper chest. They'd glisten and wave under my collar in the harsh office light, derailing my efforts to fit in with my utterly hairless male Japanese co-workers. In the U.S., the next move would've probably been body waxing and an unwise lease on a Porsche. However, because of the amazing benefits of seniority in Japan, there's no such thing as a mid-life crisis here.

It's pointless anyway to try to hide your age in a country so crowded that you can't scratch your head without elbowing somebody in the eye. Every giveaway – the greying chest hair poking out, the gut surging over your belt, the *kareishuu* middle-aged man smell – all this can be more or less concealed if you work hard at it (good luck finding time in workaholic Japan) or are blessed with the private, personal space that comes with the American car commute and office cubicle.

In Japan, where you live on those packed trains and shared office desks falling on top of each other, you age right in the face of your fellow commuters and co-workers, who sit, stand and breathe right on top of you all day. After finally grasping all this, I realized that blatantly showing your age, and touching those famous perks of Japanese seniority are where middle-aged salaryman salvation lies. Those previous, painful decades apprenticing under older Japanese managers finally start to turn in your favor once you start to hit your mid-to-late 40s, when the old age perks start to come within your view.

The following are some of these perks which, while I may have never been salaryman-enough to actually practice them, show that this is a culture that still greases its skids to the hilt for its elder males, and makes any male foreigner think twice about leaving to go be an old man back in his home country.

Perk #1: Public Napping

The older you are, the more acceptable it is to nap anytime, anywhere. Even during important business meetings, Cabinet of Japan sessions and weddings ceremonies.

I've repeatedly watched older Japanese managers doze off Grandpa Simpson-style in the middle of meeting discussions that THEY started–and everyone just let it go. In fact, if you're old enough, you're often even *given credit* for doing this in a traditional Japanese company: the typical timid, young subordinate here is programmed to take your sloth as a wise, non-verbal cue that you're happy with the meeting, that you're relaxed and not upset with them.

Perk #2: Elaborate grunting

Older people in Japan tend to grunt *"yoishou!"* whenever doing anything remotely strenuous. In the US, this is equivalent to any number of unofficial, non-word English sounds–"Ahhh", "ughhh", "humph", etc. But, of course, in Japan even personal strain is formalized: it's always *"yoishou"*, and it can be grunted softly, whispered happily with a melody, or even shouted.

It's a fogeyish add-on to a Japanese vocabulary, but I have a theory that it's also intended to work as a kind of subliminal cue to anyone listening that you're older, and thus deserving of deep respect. There's a precise style to saying *yoishou* in Japan, and it's all about timing it perfectly with whatever action is exerting you. It's common to hear old guys here go *Yoishou!* when sliding into a hot public bath, sitting down on a train seat, climbing stairs (multiple *yoishous* in this case), and I've even heard the word uttered by a guy in the men's room at his precise moment of unloading:

It's a fun word to say, and it conveys a refined, unquestioned sense of senior entitlement—for tourists over the age of 50 in Japan, try saying it in front of your Japanese hosts during your visit!

THE SALARYMAN

<u>Perk #3</u>: Leisurely post-meal use of a toothpick

There's an old Japanese proverb that says: "A samurai, even when he has not eaten, uses a toothpick like a lord". It refers to the classic, accepted older Japanese male habit of cleaning your teeth with a toothpick, but it also has a hint of honorable samurai poverty to it that conveys something about the modest pleasures of the modern, deflationary salaryman. Visit any restaurant here and you'll see that picking your teeth with a toothpick—certain to get looks of disgust in the US—harkens back to this theory of Samurai masculinity, and so it is that the modern Japanese salaryman carries on with this ancient custom. Current salaryman etiquette calls for you to cup your mouth with your hand as you pick away, like this:

Only in Japan can older men get away with these kinds of repugnant, totally self-indulgent pleasures (and I say this knowing that I would do it too if I didn't feel totally self-conscious about it). In one small office I worked in, the head guy—he was well into his 60s—would walk into the office after lunch and when his secretary greeted him with the formal "*okairi nasai*" ("welcome back"), he'd just nod, light a cigarette and say "Toothpick". To this, she'd run and fetch a toothpick for the "office samurai" to use to stab at the food stuck in his teeth.

<u>Perk #4</u>: Drinking and being drunk in public

Middle-aged or older salarymen have the public license to crack open a beer on the train home, face-plant themselves next to a *sake* bottle at bars and in general get falling-over drunk in public. Not only are they given this freedom, but they, lucky men, have the magical power to fight off hangovers through greasy bowls of late-night toxin-killing ramen and intense hot baths before bed that sweats the liquor out of their system. A hot midnight bath at home is the norm, but another source from which they draw this magical power are *sento* (local bathhouses). After drinking, some older salarymen hit the scorching *sento* pools, with their muscle-jellifying jet-blasters and exotic mineral baths.

And many take the detox up another notch at the *sento* by dipping into the *denkiburo* (electric bath). It truly tests the natural law that water and electricity should never be mixed. The *denkiburo* has oppositely-charged metallic plates attached on each side of the pool that send tiny electric currents through the water, effectively electro-shocking all those salaryman toxins out of your body. This bath is designed specifically for older people who want to stimulate blood circulation, and using it literally tests your manhood–I don't dare immerse my junk in it and can only bring myself to dip my legs in:

"電気風呂" reads as "electricity bath"

Immersed in it, you never feel more than a slightly freaky tingle, a sign of its intended benefit of increased blood flow, though the very real fear of electrocution has something to do with this too. You can sweat out almost any amount of alcohol in these *sento*, and some wise old salarymen also count on it as a kind of hangover prevention tool. I mention it only to convey something of the veneration for old age you find embedded throughout retail Japan.

Perk #5: "Descending from heaven"

Finally, as you age in a traditional Japanese company, you get increasingly venerated no matter what you do, and you live increasingly inside a cocoon of manners and ceremony. You're more like a feudal lord than a businessman. Many of the top executives at large conglomerates are treated almost like untouchable royalty, often a result of them having been sent to the company from a government post or sent after a long career at the parent company's headquarters to work as an executive at a smaller subsidiary. The men who get these close-to-retirement age transfers to exalted positions are commonly known as *amakudari* (a slightly derisive term that literally means "those descending from heaven").

One Japanese *amakudari* executive I worked for totally refused to get out of his well-mannered comfort zone to negotiate with our big American customer. He asked me to do all the behind the scenes haggling and legwork on a particularly complicated deal with them, where they'd cancelled our contract mid-stream and left us with a huge amount of wasted work-in-progress inventory. Regarding the final deal discussions, he'd only talk with them on a ceremonial level, and told me to convey to them his rules of engagement: "First handshake and agree, then make deal." He wanted them to agree in principle to a rough value on the leftover inventory (and agree not to sue us) before the final terms were done being negotiated. It was old-school Japanese style, with no confrontational deal-making. The American customer snorted back at this by email: "No way. No handshake. Must negotiate deal first." It took us 4 months to get through the deal after that, with me acting as a cultural attaché throughout.

Another instance I experienced illustrates the untouchable bubble that an *amakudari* character is allowed to operate in.

At the same company, I was once part of a key conference call with the same American customer, where we all were ordered–suddenly, without notice—to speak at a hushed, barely audible level the whole time so that we didn't disturb our *amakudari* company president in the next room. He sent his secretary into our meeting room to complain about our noise. The reason? He was filming his recorded message to employees for the company's annual report (I might add that the exalted room he was in that deserved so much respect had a view—by his design—of both the Tokyo Imperial Palace grounds and Mount Fuji). So for the rest of our call, we sat there whispering like idiots while the customer railed loudly on the other end that they couldn't hear us (worst of all, we weren't allowed to give a reason), and they ended the call after 10 minutes.

22

Getting Out

I STARTED THIS BOOK in 2016 after working at four different Japan companies during my first eight years in Japan. At some point during the three-year period I commuted two hours each way to a factory at the far edges of Tokyo city limits and where I had yet another undefined, ceremonial role and had to *shochu* Sadsack my train rides *both* ways to deal with it, I decided that maybe salaryman life really wasn't working for me.

It occurred to me that I might find a more natural fit at an American company in Japan (what a concept!), but the reality is that the vast majority of Tokyo jobs at those companies are for native Japanese who speak very good English, or American expats transferred from the U.S. headquarters for a few years. And the rare exceptions to these cases are almost always filled by local foreigners who've studied Japanese from a young age. I have to admit that much of the fuel for writing this book stemmed from my frustration at this reality.

But I finally found a job with an American company in Tokyo in 2017, and from there I parted ways with Japanese salarymanhood forever.

The Salaryman was created out of my immigrant struggle. It's a struggle I voluntarily chose and one that stemmed from my own limitations at fitting into the culture. Some of the consumption I did to get through it – the late-night company boozefests away from my young kids, my childish Bulls hooky, the Sadsacking on the trains – are not things I'm particularly proud of.

But I also learned some things that will no doubt become more useful later as I grow old, such as what the difference is between good *sake* and bad *sake* (and how to avoid gout at all costs), how to instantly take a good nap anywhere at any time, and never assuming that a nurse or doctor and I understand each other.

Over the past decade—my entire 30s—I've soaked in the middle-class Japanese experience, and all of the little retail treasures that go with it. My assimilation is at the point now that I barely notice it when an everyday Tokyo café gives me a free slice of watermelon after my meal to apologize for the inconvenience of their indoor seating being full and me having to sit in their outdoor terrace on a nice spring day.

I experienced all of this during a time of life when many white-collar Americans start to move up the salary chain fast and rack up a nice, big house with a yard, long guilt-free vacations with their family and other middle-class American goodies. The differences in the way the two cultures consume—the steady, ultra-refined, modest Japanese approach vs. American big-retail trophy hunting—are another lesson I'll take with me.

THE SALARYMAN

I superimposed Japan's set of values onto mine—namely going all-in on adopting Manner Mode—and it brought a lot of pleasure, but also a lot of regret at realizing the kind of American life I gave up in exchange. There's no doubt that the stress from this lifestyle decision helped me grow a lot as a person, nor is there any doubt that it also was a factor in the eventual breakup of my marriage to a Japanese (but that's another book altogether, with very different illustrations!). In the end, I think this is all part of the deal that many people make when they move permanently to another country.

I can only hope that my story has been interesting in the same way that a personal travel blog is interesting. I can at least say, Here is the world that awaits you if you become a salaryman in Japan. Someday, I'd like to explore that world more deeply. I'd like to understand Japanese company characters like my *sake* master and the *Robokoppu* more intimately and understand what goes on in their souls, and also learn more about what working in a Tokyo office is like from a woman's point of view. At this moment I don't feel that I've understood more than the surface of middle-class Japanese office life.

Someday I'm sure I'll look back fondly on my time as a salaryman. I'll always remember those jolly all-you-can-drink dinners with colleagues in Tokyo *izakaya*, and can point to a few more things that I've definitely learned. I'll never again think there's anything strange or wrong about a salaryman being passed-out drunk on the train, nor play a round of golf with a Japanese boss and his Korean customer, nor schedule a flight on the same day of a company health exam, nor ever again visit the Futamatagawa driver's license center. And that's a good start.

Made in the USA
Coppell, TX
16 May 2022